Louis Albert Banks, Norval Jordan

Immortal Hymns and Their Story

the narrative of the conception and striking experiences of blessing attending the

use of some of the world's greatest hymns

Louis Albert Banks, Norval Jordan

Immortal Hymns and Their Story
the narrative of the conception and striking experiences of blessing attending the use of some of the world's greatest hymns

ISBN/EAN: 9783337088958

Printed in Europe, USA, Canada, Australia, Japan

Cover: Foto ©Lupo / pixelio.de

More available books at **www.hansebooks.com**

v

IMMORTAL HYMNS
AND THEIR STORY

The Narrative of the Conception
and Striking Experiences of Blessing attending the use of some of
the WORLD'S GREATEST HYMNS

BY

Rev. Louis Albert Banks, D.D

Author of "Hero Tales from Sacred Story,"
"Christ and His Friends," "White
Slaves," etc., etc

With portraits, and illustrations by Norval Jordan

CLEVELAND: The Burrows Brothers
Company, PUBLISHERS, MDCCCXCVIII

To my friend
DR. CHARLES L. BONNELL
whose musical soul brings him into fellowship with
the singers of every age, this volume is affectionately
dedicated by the author

CONTENTS

ix

x

PORTRAITS

ILLUSTRATIONS

xiii

IN TEMPTATION.

A refuge from the storm.— Isaiah xxv., 4.

CHARLES WESLEY

MARTYN. 7. D.

SIMEON BUTLER MARSH.

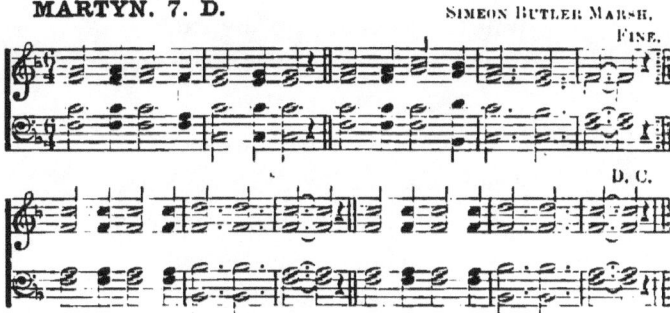

Jesus, lover of my soul,
  Let me to thy bosom fly,
While the nearer waters roll,
  While the tempest still is nigh!
Hide me, O my Saviour! hide,
  Till the storm of life is past;
Safe into the haven guide;
  O receive my soul at last!

Other refuge have I none;
  Hangs my helpless soul on thee!
Leave, ah! leave me not alone,
  Still support and comfort me!
All my trust on thee is stayed;
  All my help from thee I bring;
Cover my defenseless head
  With the shadow of thy wing!

Wilt thou not regard my call?
　Wilt thou not accept my prayer?
Lo! I sink, I faint, I fall!
　Lo! on thee I cast my care!
Reach me out thy gracious hand!
　While I of thy strength receive,
Hoping against hope I stand,
　Dying, and behold I live!

Thou, O Christ, art all I want;
　More than all in thee I find;
Raise the fallen, cheer the faint,
　Heal the sick, and lead the blind!
Just and holy is thy name,
　I am all unrighteousness,
False and full of sin I am,
　Thou art full of truth and grace.

Plenteous grace with thee is found,—
　Grace to cover all my sin;
Let the healing streams abound,
　Make and keep me pure within.
Thou of life the fountain art;
　Freely let me take of thee;
Spring thou up within my heart;
　Rise to all eternity.

　　　　　　　　—*Charles Wesley.*

Many accounts are given of the immediate circumstances of the writing of this, the most famous

...Let me to thy bosom fly

of Charles Wesley's hymns, and one of the most popular in the English tongue. One account is that the poet was standing one day at a window, when a hawk pursued a little bird so closely that it flew against the pane, losing its fear of man in the greater danger which threatened; and Wesley, opening the lattice, took it in out of peril, and turned away and wrote this hymn. This story probably arose from the imagery of the opening lines in the first and second verses,—

> " Jesus, lover of my soul,
>   Let me to thy bosom fly;"

and,—

> " Other refuge have I none."

It is quite probable, however, that the hymn had its inspiration on the sea. But a short time before writing it, Mr. Wesley had narrowly escaped shipwreck in a storm on the Atlantic, and the words, taken as a whole, seem to indicate that this was the vision before his mind. This is peculiarly true of the first verse,—

> " While the nearer waters roll,
>   While the tempest still is nigh!"

And again, in the closing lines,—

> " Safe into the haven guide:
>   O receive my soul at last!"

In the third verse, which is usually omitted in the hymnals, in the lines,—

> " Lo! I sink, I faint, I fall!
>   Lo! on thee I cast my care!
> Reach me out thy gracious hand!
>   While I of thy strength receive,
> Hoping against hope I stand,
>   Dying, and behold I live!"

there is an unmistakable reference to the graphic imagery of Matthew's story of Peter's attempt to walk on the Sea of Galilee, which, to a mind like Charles Wesley's, would naturally be suggested, when viewing the turbulent waves from the deck of a tempest-tossed sailing vessel.

Among the interesting stories which show the striking circumstances in which this hymn has given comfort, is this: On the rocky coast of Wales a company on shore were watching a ship going to pieces on the rocks. At last they descried, still clinging to the broken vessel, a single sailor. There was no chance to save him, as no boat could live in the rough sea. They brought a speaking-trumpet, hoping to convey to him some message. They handed it to the old village preacher. He wondered what to say. He thought over his sermons, but could think of only one thing appropriate — but one thing that he dared to utter at such a time. Raising the trumpet to his lips, he shouted, " Look to Jesus!

Can you hear?" And back came the faint answer, almost drowned by the noise of the winds and waves, "Aye! aye! sir." Then, as they watched and listened, some one exclaimed, " He is singing!" And to their strained ears there came over the waves the murmur of the lines, —

> " Jesus, lover of my soul,
>   Let me to thy bosom fly."

And it thrilled them as again faintly they heard, —

> " While the nearer waters' roll,
>   While the tempest still is nigh!"

Then, fainter still, —

> " Safe into the haven guide;
>   O receive my soul at last!"

Fainter yet came the opening of the next verse, —

> " Other refuge have I none;
>   Hangs my helpless soul on thee'"

Then his frail hold on the broken wreck gave way, and the singer dropped into the sea; while on shore they said, " He passed to be with Jesus in the singing of that hymn."

THE PILLAR OF CLOUD.

He took not away the pillar of the cloud by day, nor the pillar of fire by night, from before the people.— Exodus xiii., 22.

JOHN HENRY NEWMAN

LUX BENIGNA. 10, 4, 10.   Rev. John Baccus Dykes.

Lead, kindly Light, amid the encircling gloom,
    Lead thou me on;
The night is dark, and I am far from home,
    Lead thou me on.
Keep thou my feet; I do not ask to see
The distant scene; one step enough for me.

I was not ever thus, nor prayed that thou
    Shouldst lead me on;
I loved to choose and see my path; but now
    Lead thou me on.
I loved the garish day, and, spite of fears,
Pride ruled my will: remember not past years.

So long thy power hath blest me, sure it still
  Will lead me on
O'er moor and fen, o'er crag and torrent, till
  The night is gone.
And with the morn those angel faces smile
Which I have loved long since, and lost awhile.

> —*John Henry Newman.*

Cardinal Newman's beautiful hymn was the outcome of a long and painful mental and spiritual
struggle. It is surely remarkable that a man who
wrote so many books, and who filled so large a
place in the intellectual and religious life of more
than two generations, should be remembered more
by one hymn of three stanzas than on account of
all else whatsoever. The struggle through which
he passed prior to entering into the restfulness suggested by this hymn is described by some other
verses, written but a little earlier: —

" Time was I shrank from what was right,
  From fear of what was wrong;
I would not brave the sacred fight,
  Because the foe was strong.

" But now I cast that finer sense
  And sorer shame aside;
Such dread of sin was indolence,
  Such aim at heaven was pride.

32

" So, when my Saviour calls, I rise,
  And calmly do my best;
Leaving to him, with silent eyes,
  Of hope and fear the rest.

" I step, I mount, where he has led;
  Men count my haltings o'er; —
I know them; yet, though self I dread,
  I love his precept more."

In June, 1833, Dr. Newman was sailing on the Mediterranean, in an orange boat, coming home from Sicily, where he had long been ill with malarial fever. He says of the voyage that he was writing verses nearly the entire time of the trip. On the sixteenth of June the slow sailing boat of fragrant freight was lying in the Straits of Bonifacio, between Corsica and Sardinia. They had been becalmed for a week; and if any one has ever been becalmed at sea when anxious to get home, he will understand the great demand for patience which is made by such an experience. "Aching" to be at home, as he expressed it, having made up his mind as to his future, and yet unable to see the outcome, the great preacher-poet penned the verses of this immortal hymn.

If one will re-read the hymn, keeping in mind the becalmed ship, so like his own becalmed mind, after a long struggle, pausing before a tempestuous

35

voyage, it is full of meaning not discovered before.

If I were to rename this hymn, I would call it "The Pilgrim's Hymn." I do not know any song, ancient or modern, that with such combined tenderness, pathos, and faith tells the story of the Christian pilgrim who walks by faith and not by sight. No doubt it is this fidelity to heart experience, common to us all, that makes the hymn such a universal favorite. There are dark nights, and homesick hours, and becalmed seas for each of us, in which it is natural for man to cry out in Newman's words, —

" The night is dark, and I am far from home,
Lead thou me on."

And who of us does not look back on times of self-will, when the " garish day " fascinated us, and led us astray, and find a very appropriate prayer and confession in the line, —

" Pride ruled my will: remember not past years."

But I apprehend that it is the gleam of hope — undying, invincible hope — in the last verse which has seized hold of the heart of mankind in every land; for whatever failures life may have had for us, however broken into fragments the ambitions of youth, Christ causes hope to spring immortal in the human breast, and a remembrance of Divine mercy in the

36

past encourages the tempted and stained and travel-
worn pilgrim to sing,—

" So long thy power hath blest me, sure it still
      Will lead me on
  O'er moor and fen, o'er crag and torrent, till
      The night is gone.
  And with the morn those angel faces smile
  Which I have loved long since, and lost awhile. ''

ABIDE WITH ME.

Abide with us: for it is toward evening, and the day is far spent.— Luke xxiv., 29.

"Abide with me! fast falls the eventide"

EVENTIDE. 10.   William Henry Monk.

Abide with me! fast falls the eventide;
The darkness deepens; Lord, with me abide!
When other helpers fail, and comforts flee,
Help of the helpless, O abide with me!

Swift to its close ebbs out Life's little day;
Earth's joys grow dim; its glories pass away;
Change and decay in all around I see:
O thou, who changest not, abide with me!

Not a brief glance I beg, a passing word,
But, as thou dwell'st with thy disciples, Lord,
Familiar, condescending, patient, free,
Come, not to sojourn, but abide with me!

Come not in terrors, as the King of kings,
But kind and good, with healing in thy wings,
Tears for all woes, a heart for every plea,
Come, Friend of sinners, and thus 'bide with me!

Thou on my head in early youth didst smile;
And, though rebellious and perverse meanwhile,
Thou hast not left me, oft as I left thee,
On to the close, O Lord, abide with me!

I need thy presence every passing hour;
What but thy grace can foil the tempter's power?
Who like thyself my guide and stay can be?
Through cloud and sunshine, O abide with me!

I fear no foe with thee at hand to bless;
Ills have no weight, and tears no bitterness.
Where is Death's sting? Where, Grave, thy victory?
I triumph still, if thou abide with me!

Hold then thy cross before my closing eyes;
Shine through the gloom, and point me to the skies;
Heaven's morning breaks, and earth's vain shadows flee;
In life, in death, O Lord, abide with me!
                              —*Henry Francis Lyte.*

This glorious hymn, which has taken to itself
wings and crossed all oceans, transcending all the
boundaries of race and speech, and comforting
humanity in all lands, had a most interesting birth.
Perhaps none of the great hymns of the Christian
faith have a more fascinating story connected with
the circumstances of their authorship.

Henry Francis Lyte was destined to make the voyage of life in a frail and sickly body, and all his life long he had to think of the effect of climate and surroundings upon his delicate health. To make his case still harder, he was always poor, and poverty and sickness wrought together in the development of his character; yet so gentle and submissive was his spirit that these afflictions only brought into finer display the graces of a Christian life.

In one of his poems, which he says sprang from "Thoughts in Weakness," and which he entitles "Submission," he sings with spiritual insight and courage: —

> " And shall I murmur or repine
>   At aught thy hand may send?
> To whom should I my cause resign,
>   If not to such a friend?
> Where love and wisdom deign to choose,
>   Shall I the choice condemn,
> Or dare the medicine to refuse
>   That is prescribed by them?
>
> " As woods, when shaken by the breeze,
>   Take deeper, firmer root;
> As winter's frosts but make the trees
>   Abound in summer fruit;
> So every heaven-sent pang and throe
>   That Christian firmness tries,
> But nerves us for our work below,
>   And forms us for the skies."

The gentle poet — for he was always more a poet than preacher — toiled for more than twenty years at Brixham, a fishing town, full of hardy sailors and hard-working, weather-beaten fishermen. He was greatly devoted to his pastoral labors, and composed hymns to sing about the fisher's cottage, and to sing from the decks of their venturesome little boats; and others for his own comfort and consolation. Many of his songs, like the one which has made his fame universal, are distilled from his own heart experience. Where else could a hymn like this have had its source? —

> " My spirit on thy care,
>   Blest Saviour, I recline;
> Thou wilt not leave me to despair,
>   For thou art love divine.
>
> ' In thee I place my trust,
>   On thee I calmly rest;
> I know thee good, I know thee just,
>   And count thy choice the best.
>
> " Whate'er events betide,
>   Thy will they all perform;
> Safe in thy breast my head I hide,
>   Nor fear the coming storm.
>
> " Let good or ill befall,
>   It must be good for me;
> Secure of having thee in all,
>   Of having all in thee."

But after a while, though only forty-seven years old, it was seen that his brave fight against that insidious foe of the human body, consumption, was in vain; and that only a radical change of climate could prolong, even for a little time, his loving and useful life. At this time he was filled, as many another has been under similar circumstances, with a great longing to use his failing powers in some service for humanity. This longing is voiced with wonderful pathos in a poem entitled " Declining Days," in which he shows us the secret throbbings of his gentle heart: —

" Might verse of mine inspire
　　One virtuous aim, one high resolve impart;
　Light in one drooping soul a hallowed fire,
　　Or bind one broken heart,

" Death would be sweeter then,
　　More calm my slumber 'neath the silent sod;
　Might I thus live to bless my fellow-men,
　　Or glorify my God."

Nothing could be more pathetic than the prayer with which he closes this poem in which he unveils his secret heart: —

" O thou, whose touch can lend
　　Life to the dead, thy quickening grace supply;
　And grant me, swan-like, my last breath to spend
　　In song that may not die."

47

The prayer of this verse, for a swan song that should perpetuate him in loving service for his Master, was most graciously answered. It was in the autumn when his friends and physician insisted on his going away to a more genial clime, and thus grasp the last opportunity for improved health. He went once more to his pulpit to deliver his farewell sermon to his congregation of sobbing, broken-hearted fishermen and their families. After administering to them the Lord's Supper, he went home tired and worn in body, but exalted in spirit. For the last time the fire of poetic inspiration burned high in his soul, and in the light of it, as the light faded out of the sky on that Sunday evening along the Brixham Coast, he wrote his never-dying hymn, —

" Abide with me! fast falls the eventide."

A LIVING AND DYING PRAYER FOR THE
HOLIEST BELIEVER IN
THE WORLD.

As the shadow of a great rock in a weary land.
— Isaiah xxxii., 2.

A LIVING AND DYING PRAYER FOR THE HOLIEST BELIEVER IN THE WORLD.

TOPLADY. 7, 61.

THOMAS HASTINGS

Rock of Ages, cleft for me,
Let me hide myself in thee!
Let the water and the blood,
From thy riven side which flowed,
Be of sin the double cure,
Cleanse me from its guilt and power.

Not the labour of my hands
Can fulfill thy law's demands;
Could my zeal no respite know,
Could my tears forever flow,
All for sin could not atone;
Thou must save, and thou alone.

Nothing in my hand I bring;
Simply to thy cross I cling;

Naked, come to thee for dress;
Helpless, look to thee for grace;
Foul, I to the Fountain fly;
Wash me, Saviour, or I die.

While I draw this fleeting breath,
When my eyestrings break in death,
When I soar through tracts unknown,
See thee on thy judgment throne,—
Rock of Ages, cleft for me,
Let me hide myself in thee!

—*Augustus Montague Toplady.*

Toplady wrote this hymn, which vies with Charles Wesley's "Jesus, Lover of My Soul" in being the most universally popular hymn in the English tongue, while dying of consumption, at thirty-six years of age. This knowledge makes especially pathetic the title which he gave the hymn. His thought was that the holiest person in the world must say in his prayer, "Thou must save, and thou alone."

Mr. Gladstone, easily the first private citizen of the world, has made a version of this hymn in Latin, and another in Greek. Many distinguished people have used it as a dying prayer, among whom was Prince Albert, the lamented husband of Queen Victoria.

Mrs. Lucy Seaman Bainbridge tells the story of an old Chinese woman, who had sought to "make merit " for herself by digging with awful labor a well twenty-five feet deep and some ten or fifteen feet across. The poor old woman had dug out every inch of it with her frail, weak hands, hoping by this self-torture to escape the painful transmigrations of the next life. But all this brought her no peace, and she found no rest for her soul until she learned of Christ and of the free Gospel of salvation. She was eighty years of age when Mrs. Bainbridge saw her, but she stretched out her crippled fingers, and with trembling voice sang with her visitor,—

" Nothing in my hand I bring,
Simply to thy cross I cling."

When the steamship *London* was lost in the Bay of Biscay in 1866, the last man who escaped said that when he left the ship the passengers were singing,—

" Rock of Ages, cleft for me,
Let me hide myself in thee."

A few years ago a vessel was on fire in New York harbor, and before help could come the passengers were all forced into the water. There was on board a noted public singer, with his wife. Just as he was fastening a life preserver about his wi half-crazed with fright rushed by and jerk his grasp. The flames drove them in. into the water. The man was a strong swimmer, and by his wife clinging to his shoulders he managed to keep both her and himself from drowning, but at last she said: " I can hold on no longer. I shall have to give up." In his awful agony the husband grasped at the one straw of hope that came to his mind; he said calmly, " Let us sing," and struck up,—

" Rock of Ages, cleft for me."

His wife joined him, and seemed to gain strength from the hymn. There were about them over a hundred others struggling for life in the mocking glare of the burning ship, and many of them joined in the song, until the grand old anthem of trust and confidence in the divine Savior went up from half a hundred throats. Some of them went down to rise no more, with the precious words on their lips; but many others lived to bear testimony that they were given strength to hold out by the inspiration of the song.

Toplady himself died in full and joyous confidence in the " Rock of Ages " of which he sang. His physician, examining him one day, said, " Your pulse is becoming weaker."

"   ' is a good sign," said the poet, " that my
            t approaching; and I can add that my
            every day stronger and stronger for

And when his physician sought to encourage him

"Rock of Ages, cleft for me"

to believe that he would live some time longer, he replied: " No, no; I shall die, for no mortal could endure such manifestations of God's glory as I have had, and live."

His last hymn is full of the confidence of the greater song which has made his name immortal: —

" When languor and disease invade
  This trembling house of clay,
 'Tis sweet to look beyond my pains,
  And long to fly away;

" Sweet to look inward, and attend
  The whispers of his love;
Sweet to look upward to the place
  Where Jesus pleads above;

" Sweet to look back, and see my name
  In life's fair book set down;
Sweet to look forward, and behold
  Eternal joys my own;

" Sweet to reflect how grace divine
  My sins on Jesus laid;
Sweet to remember that his blood
  My debt of suffering paid;

" Sweet to rejoice in lively hope,
  That, when my change shall come,
Angels shall hover round my bed,
  And waft my spirit home.

" If such the sweetness of the stream,
    What must the fountain be,
  Where saints and angels draw their bliss
    Directly, Lord, from thee."

A PROSPECT OF HEAVEN MAKES DEATH EASY.

For he looked for a city which hath foundations, whose builder and maker is God.— Hebrews xi., 10.

ISAAC WATTS

A PROSPECT OF HEAVEN MAKES DEATH EASY.

VARINA. C. M.   JOHANN CHRISTIAN HEINRICH RINK.

There is a land of pure delight,
  Where saints immortal reign,
Infinite day excludes the night,
  And pleasures banish pain.

There everlasting spring abides,
  And never-withering flowers;
Death, like a narrow sea, divides
  This heavenly land from ours.

Sweet fields beyond the swelling flood
  Stand dressed in living green:
So to the Jews old Canaan stood,
  While Jordan rolled between.

But timorous mortals start and shrink
    To cross this narrow sea,
And linger shivering on the brink,
    And fear to launch away.

Oh, could we make our doubts remove,
    These gloomy doubts that rise,
And see the Canaan that we love
    With unbeclouded eyes,—

Could we but climb where Moses stood,
    And view the landscape o'er,—
Not Jordan's stream nor death's cold flood
    Should fright us from the shore!

                —*Isaac Watts.*

During the reign of the second Stuart, a Puritan dissenter of Southampton, England, was confined in jail because of his faith. This heroic young Christian had a beautiful wife who used to come to the jail every day, with her baby boy in her arms, and spend hours in singing for the comfort of her husband. That little babe was Isaac Watts, and he seems to have inherited his mother's love of music.

When young Watts was eighteen years of age, he became greatly disgusted with the ungraceful and ugly rhymes which were used in the church where he attended. On a Sunday morning when the singing had been worse than usual, the boy stepped up to one of the church officials and expressed his con-

tempt for the miserable doggerel. In those days youngsters were expected to keep silent in regard to such matters, and the church elder sternly regarded him, and said: "Give us something better then, young man!" The disgusted lad went home and set himself to work to accept the challenge. Before sunset he had written a hymn which was lined off and sung at the evening service. The first verse was as follows: —

> " Behold the glories of the Lamb,
>   Amidst his father's throne;
> Prepare new honors for his name
>   And songs before unknown."

He was sitting, one spring day, at his window in Southampton, looking out across the river Itchen. Beyond the narrow river was the Isle of Wight, marvelously picturesque and beautiful in the full glory of its spring coloring. It was one of those lovely days when there is gladness in simply being alive, and as he drew in the fresh air, and his eyes feasted on the beauties of harbor and river, and field and forest, his thought led him on to consider that if God had made so beautiful this world in which we were to spend so short a period, how much more glorious must be the heavenly world which is to be the scene of an immortal career. To Isaac Watts every such conception naturally crystallized into song, and he soon embodied the beautiful thought

into the sweetest of all his hymns. As we read it
with this story of its birth in our mind, the imagery
which inspired it is constantly recalled,—

" There is a land of pure delight,
    Where saints immortal reign,
Infinite day excludes the night,
    And pleasures banish pain."

And as the hymn proceeds, the picture from the
poet's window reappears throughout the verses,—

" There everlasting spring abides,
    And never-withering flowers;
Death, like a narrow sea, divides
    This heavenly land from ours.

" Sweet fields beyond the swelling flood
    Stand dressed in living green:
So to the Jews old Canaan stood,
    While Jordan rolled between."

It is related that during the Crimean War, on a
bitterly cold night, a poor soldier was suffering such
agonies from hunger and cold that he had made up
his mind to commit suicide, and thus seek to end his
sufferings, when suddenly he heard a voice singing,—

" There is a land of pure delight."

The hymn inspired him with hope, and he called

out loudly. The singer, a good man who had lost
his way in the storm and was cheering himself on
his lonely journey by singing, heard him, and made
his way to him through the snow. He proved a
friend in need to the despairing soldier.

Many a soul has stood with Isaac Watts on the
mount of spiritual vision under the inspiration of
the last verse of his great hymn,—

> " Could we but climb where Moses stood,
>   And view the landscape o'er,—
> Not Jordan's stream nor death's cold flood
>   Should fright us from the shore! "

71

MISSIONARY HYMN.

Go ye into all the world, and preach the gospel to every creature.— Mark xvi., 15.

REGINALD HEBER

MISSIONARY HYMN. 7, 6.   LOWELL MASON.

From Greenland's icy mountains,
　From India's coral strand,
Where Afric's sunny fountains
　Roll down their golden sand,
From many an ancient river,
　From many a palmy plain,
They call us to deliver
　Their land from error's chain.

What though the spicy breezes
　Blow soft o'er Ceylon's isle,—
Though every prospect pleases,
　And only man is vile?

77

In vain with lavish kindness
    The gifts of God are strown;
The heathen in his blindness
    Bows down to wood and stone.

Can we, whose souls are lighted
    With wisdom from on high,
Can we to men benighted
    The lamp of life deny?
Salvation, O salvation!
    The joyful sound proclaim,
Till each remotest nation
    Has learnt Messiah's name.

Waft, waft, ye winds, his story,
    And you, ye waters, roll,
Till like a sea of glory
    It spreads from pole to pole;
Till o'er our ransomed nature
    The Lamb for sinners slain,
Redeemer, King, Creator,
    In bliss returns to reign.

                —*Reginald Heber.*

Very rarely indeed does one who performs great deeds know the value of his work at the time. The greatest work men accomplish is not the deed that is done in the spirit of labor, but rather that which is performed in a buoyant spirit which makes it a work of love. The greatest poems have been written under the inspiration of an occasion, and their author has not dreamed that in them was his own title to immortality.

Reginald Heber, the poet-bishop of India, was as yet only the rector of an Episcopal church in Shropshire, England. He was but thirty-six years old, and was on a visit to his father-in-law, a certain Dr. Shipley, vicar of Wrexham, on the border of Wales. The vicar had invited his son-in-law to deliver the first of a series of Sunday evening missionary lectures in his church. It was Saturday afternoon, and the poet-preacher sat in the parlor with his father-in-law and a few friends, enjoying a pleasant conversation. Suddenly Dr. Shipley, remembering the young man's gift of verse-making, turned to him and said, " Reginald, write something for us to sing at the service to-morrow." Heber immediately excused himself and, drawing his chair to another part of the room, began to scribble on a little slip of paper. The Dean and his friends went on conversing. When there came a lull in the conversation, the host turned to his son-in-law, and noting that he seemed to be meditating on what he had already composed, inquired: " What have you written?" Heber had then completed the first three verses, and read them over. Dr. Shipley listened, and coolly replied, when the reading ceased, " There, there, that will do very well."

" No, no; the sense is not complete," replied the

poet; and he proceeded to add the fourth verse, which has been the bugle-blast of missions ever since, —

" Waft, waft, ye winds, his story,
    And you, ye waters, roll,
    Till like a sea of glory
    It spreads from pole to pole;
    Till o'er our ransomed nature
    The Lamb for sinners slain,
    Redeemer, King. Creator,
    In bliss returns to reign."

Heber was anxious to add another verse, and pleaded, " Let me add another! O let me add another!" But his father-in-law would not hear to it, and declared another verse would spoil it; and so the hymn was left just as we have it now, except the alteration of a single word. The seventh line of the second verse was, —

" The *savage* in his blindness."

The author erased the word " savage" and substituted for it the more appropriate word " heathen." The hymn was printed on the same evening it was written, and was sung the next morning in the Wrexham church. As another has well said, little did the young English rector dream, as he listened to his lines sung that Sabbath morning, that he was

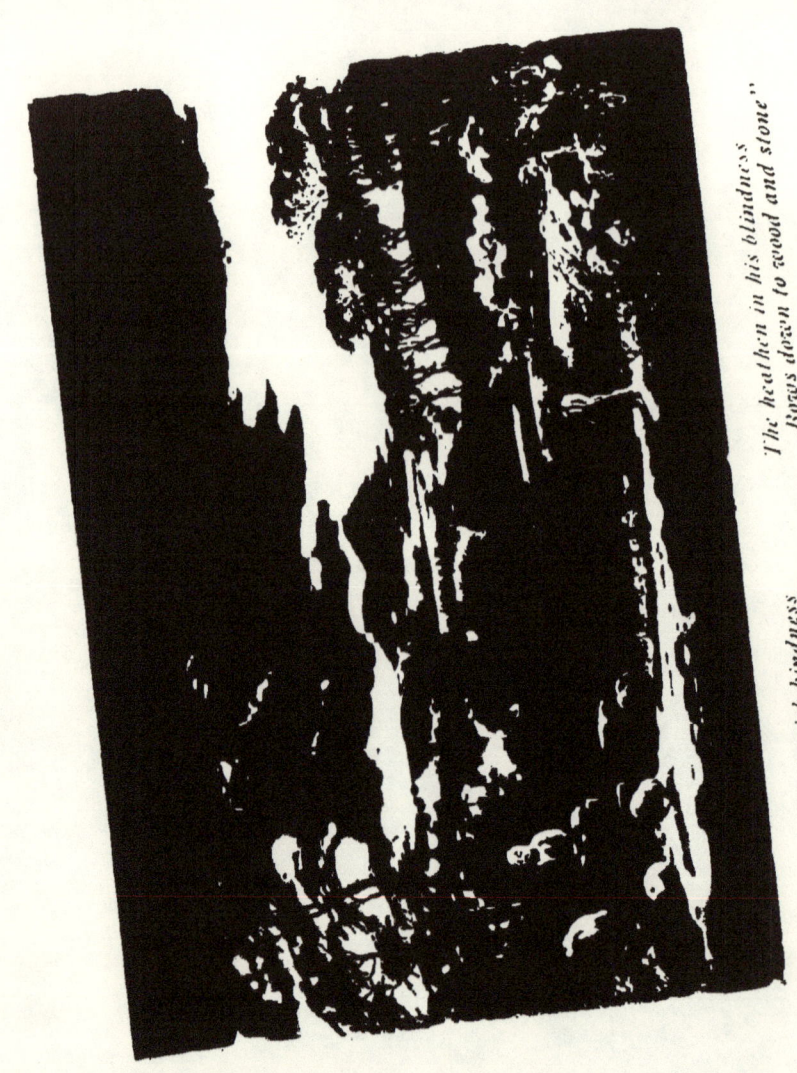

"In vain with lavish kindness
The gifts of God are strowen:

The heathen in his blindness
Bows down to wood and stone"

catching the first strains of his own immortality. That trumpet hymn is the martial music to which Christ's hosts " keep step " as they advance to the conquest of the globe.

Heber lived but seven years after the composition of his masterpiece. In June, 1823, he left England for Calcutta, as the Missionary Bishop of India. There is a very interesting passage in his *Journal of a Voyage to India*, printed long after his death, in which he comments on the beautiful lines in the second verse of his great hymn,—

" What though the spicy breezes
  Blow soft o'er Ceylon's isle."

Under date of September 23, 1823, he writes: " Though we were now too far off Ceylon to catch the odors of the land, yet it is, we are assured, perfectly true that such odors are perceptible to a very considerable distance. In the Straits of Malacca, a smell like that of a hawthorne hedge is commonly experienced; and from Ceylon at thirty or forty miles, under certain circumstances, a yet more agreeable scent is inhaled."

Heber had the true missionary spirit, and his hymn was but the outflow of his heart's feeling. It was true of him that he could not —

" .   .   .   .   to men benighted
  The lamp of life deny."

83

One of the most interesting occasions connected with the singing of this hymn was that of a revival of religion on the United States Frigate *North Carolina*, in 1858. A number of converted sailors were one day comparing nationalities, and found that they came from ten different countries; and when the last man stated that he had been born in Greenland, one of the others began to sing,—

" From Greenland's icy mountains,"

all joining in the song with tearful joy.

LIGHT SHINING OUT OF DARKNESS.

Verily, thou art a God that hidest thyself.—
Isaiah xlv., 15.

WILLIAM COWPER

MANOAH. C. M. From Mehul and Haydn.

God moves in a mysterious way,
  His wonders to perform;
He plants his footsteps in the sea,
  And rides upon the storm.

Deep in unfathomable mines
  Of never-failing skill
He treasures up his bright designs,
  And works his sovereign will.

Ye fearful saints, fresh courage take;
  The clouds ye so much dread
Are big with mercy, and shall break
  In blessings on your head.

Judge not the Lord by feeble sense,
  But trust him for his grace;

Behind a frowning providence
    He hides a smiling face.

His purposes will ripen fast,
    Unfolding every hour;
The bud may have a bitter taste,
    But sweet will be the flower.

Blind unbelief is sure to err,
    And scan his work in vain;
God is his own interpreter,
    And he will make it plain.

                    —William Cowper.

James T. Fields, the Boston littérateur, the companion of poets all his life, declared that to be the author of such a hymn as this masterpiece of Cowper was an achievement that "angels themselves might envy."

William Cowper was a man who went through life with a broken heart. In early life he formed a very deep attachment for his cousin, a lovely young woman, to whom he gave all his heart's affection; they were engaged to be married, but their union was made impossible by the action of his father. This deep disappointment was supposed to have been largely the cause of the melancholy under the heavy shadow of which he spent many years of his long life. He was one of those gentle, sensitive souls to whom heartbreak is possible. This fineness of spirit is very beautifully illustrated in his affection for his mother. It was his great misfortune to lose her by death when he was but a child five years of age. When he was nearly sixty years a picture of her was sent him by a friend. On looking at it all his childish memories were revived, and one of the most beautiful of his poems is that on his " Mother's Picture." What could be more charming than this verse! —

" Oh, that those lips had language! life has passed
With me but roughly since I heard thee last.
Those lips are thine: thy own sweet smile I see,—
The same that oft in childhood solaced me."

He wrote to the friend who had afforded him so much pleasure by sending him the picture: " I had rather possess my mother's picture than the richest jewel in the British crown; for I loved her with an affection that her death, fifty years since, has not in the least abated."

The heavy gloom of threatened insanity was the inspiration of many of his songs. The last poem he ever wrote, " The Castaway," is perhaps, under all the circumstances, one of the most heartbreaking ever composed. The poet had been reading in Anson's *Voyages*, the story of a man lost overboard in a storm. In graphic verse he tells of the hapless fate of the poor sailor, and then paints his own fate in darker colors: —

" No poet wept him; but the page of narrative sin-
cere,
That tells his name, his worth, his age, is wet
with Anson's tear;
And tears, by bards or heroes shed,
Alike immortalize the dead.

" I therefore purpose not, or dream descanting on
his fate,
To give the melancholy theme a more enduring
date;
But misery still delights to trace
Its semblance in another's case.

" No voice Divine the storm allayed, no light propi-
tious shone,
When, snatched from all effectual aid, we perished
each alone;
But I beneath a rougher sea,
And whelmed in deeper gulfs than he!"

The melancholy which had cast such a shadow
over his early manhood had been for a long time
largely lightened. For seven years he had been
comparatively cheerful. It is easy to imagine the
anguish with which he detected the return of that
shadow, worse than death. As these black clouds
of despair gathered about him again, threatening to
shut out the light of hope, he came to believe that
it was the Divine will that he should go to a par-

"He plants his footsteps in the sea,
And rides upon the storm"

ticular part of the river Ouse, and drown himself. Fortunately, the driver of the post-chaise missed his way, and he was thus diverted from his purpose. On his return home he wrote this splendid hymn, —

" God moves in a mysterious way,
    His wonders to perform;
He plants his footsteps in the sea,
    And rides upon the storm."

It was surely a wonderful triumph of faith that could inspire the afflicted poet, under such circumstances, to send forth such strains of good cheer, —

" Judge not the Lord by feeble sense,
    But trust him for his grace;
Behind a frowning providence
    He hides a smiling face."

This sweet hymn of providence has been a God-given " song in the night " to millions of tried and troubled souls all around the globe. During the terrible famine in Lancashire, England, the work ran low at one of the great cotton mills. Occupation and wages grew less day by day. At length the overseer met the half-starved operatives and announced to them the fatal tidings, " There is no more work." As their glimmering hopes went out in the darkness of despair, a delicate, sweet girl, herself pale and worn with insufficient food, stood up in the midst of the despairing company and began to sing the trustful words from Cowper's hymn, —

" Ye fearful saints, fresh courage take;
    The clouds ye so much dread
Are big with mercy, and shall break
    In blessings on your head.

" Blind unbelief is sure to err,
    And scan his work in vain;
God is his own interpreter,
    And he will make it plain."

The sentiment of the song, given magnetic power by the pure personality of the young girl, brought hope to the hearts of both employers and working people. The hymn proved a prophecy. The proprietors determined to struggle on for a while longer, and it was not long before the mill was running again on full time, and there was work and plenty for all.

GERHARDT'S HYMN OF TRUST.

*Commit thy way unto the Lord; trust also in him;
and he shall bring it to pass.* — Psalm xxxvii., 5.

PAUL GERHARDT

SCHUMANN. S. M.   ROBERT SCHUMANN.

Commit thou all thy griefs
  And ways into his hands,
To his sure trust and tender care
  Who earth and heaven commands.

Who points the clouds their course,
  Whom winds and seas obey,
He shall direct thy wandering feet,
  He shall prepare thy way.

Thou on the Lord rely,
  So, safe, shalt thou go on;
Fix on his work thy steadfast eye,
  So shall thy work be done.

No profit canst thou gain
  By self-consuming care;
To him commend thy cause; his ear
  Attends the softest prayer.

Thy everlasting truth,
  Father, thy ceaseless love,
Sees all thy children's wants, and knows
  What best for each will prove.

Thou everywhere hast sway,
  And all things serve thy might;
Thy every act pure blessing is,
  Thy path unsullied light.

Give to the winds thy fears,
  Hope, and be undismayed;
God hears thy sighs and counts thy tears;
  God shall lift up thy head.

Through waves, and clouds, and storms,
  He gently clears thy way;
Wait thou his time, so shall this night
  Soon end in joyous day.

Still heavy is thy heart?
  Still sink thy spirits down?
Cast off the weight, let fear depart,
  And every care be gone.

What though thou rulest not,
  Yet heaven and earth and hell
Proclaim: " God sitteth on the throne,
  And ruleth all things well."

Leave to his sovereign sway
  To choose and to command:

So shalt thou, wondering, own his way,
How wise, how strong his hand!

Far, far above thy thought
His counsel shall appear,
When fully he the work hath wrought
That caused thy needless fear.

—*Paul Gerhardt.*
(Translated by John Wesley.)

The sweet story of Christian trust and confidence out of which this hymn was born is of the greatest interest. The story has been denied by some recent writers, but as it is still relied upon by the majority of German Christians, is borne out by the hymn itself, and is, above all, good enough to be true, I think it well to let it go on its way of comfort and good cheer.

In 1666, Paul Gerhardt, who had been pastor of the Nicholai Church at Berlin, was removed from his place on account of his firm adherence to the Lutheran doctrines. He had been pastor there for ten years, and it was with the tenderest sorrow that he went into exile. He had a lovely and amiable wife, and his trials were greatly increased because his reverses deprived her of the comforts and luxuries to which she had been accustomed. Driven from the country by the order of the king, he turned his face toward Saxony, which was his native land. So reduced in circumstances was he at the time that, accompanied by his wife, he undertook the journey on foot. One day, as evening drew near, they turned aside from the highway to seek rest and food in a little village inn. The wife of the poet was so overcome with sorrow that she gave way to sobs and tears of anguish. Gerhardt's own heart was heavy, but concealing as best as he could his own sorrow, he quoted to her the beautiful promise of the Psalmist: "Trust in the Lord; in all thy ways acknowledge him, and he shall direct thy paths." And as the tears still flowed, he added still another quotation: "Commit thy way unto the Lord; trust also in him; and he shall bring it to pass. And he shall bring forth thy righteousness as the light, and thy judgment as the noonday."

Though these Scriptures did not, at the time, bring the comfort he desired to the heart of his wife, Gerhardt received the blessing which often comes to those who are trying to help others, in that his own heart was greatly soothed and encouraged by the Scriptures he had quoted. Passing into a little garden connected with the inn, he paused in an arbor for prayer. His devotions roused his soul to poetic flight, and with the Scripture he had quoted to his wife still in his thought, he took a slip of paper from his pocket and began writing his famous "Hymn of Trust," which gains new interest as we read it in the light of this story, —

"He shall direct thy wandering feet.
He shall prepare thy way"

" Commit thou all thy griefs
 And ways into his hands,
  To his sure trust and tender care
   Who earth and heaven commands.

" Who points the clouds their course,
 Whom winds and seas obey,
  He shall direct thy wandering feet,
   He shall prepare thy way."

Having written the first eight verses, he returned
to the inn to find his wife still prostrated by her
grief. Deeply impressed by the sight, he sat down
in another part of the room and composed the four
remaining stanzas,—

" Still heavy is thy heart?
 Still sink thy spirits down?
  Cast off the weight, let fear depart,
   And every care be gone.

" What though thou rulest not,
 Yet heaven and earth and hell
  Proclaim: ' God sitteth on the throne
   And ruleth all things well.'

" Leave to his sovereign sway
 To choose and to command,
  So shalt thou, wondering, own his way,
   How wise, how strong his hand!

" Far, far above thy thought
His counsel shall appear,
When fully he the work hath wrought
That caused thy needless fear."

Late that evening, as Gerhardt and his wife were
conversing together in the little parlor of the inn,
two belated travelers came in, and after some general conversation remarked incidentally that they
were going to Berlin to see Paul Gerhardt, the de-
posed minister. Madame Gerhardt was greatly
alarmed, fearing that some new calamity was about
to befall them; but her husband immediately answered, "I am Paul Gerhardt." One of the gen-
tlemen then handed him an autograph letter from
Duke Christian of Merseburg, which informed him
that a pension had been settled upon him for life,
and invited him to make that city his home. Gerhardt, in the great joy of the occasion, quietly
turned to his wife, and handed her the hymn he
had composed earlier in the evening, when all was
so dark and seemingly so hopeless. "See," said the
poet, "how God provides! Did I not bid you confide in him and all would be well?"

One of the most interesting and historic occasions
on which this hymn has been used, was on the first
march of the Woman's Crusade, at Hillsboro, Ohio.
The women had met in a little church, and decided
to go out into the town and talk with the liquor

dealers, and try to persuade them to cease selling a beverage that caused so much sorrow and misery. When they were ready to start they fell into line, two and two, the shorter women marching at the head and the taller bringing up the rear. As they began their march, they commenced singing a stanza of Gerhardt's hymn,—

" Give to the winds thy fears;
    Hope, and be undismayed;
God hears thy sighs and counts thy tears;
    God shall lift up thy head."

And as they passed down into the street these prophetic words floated out on the air, borne on the wings of their reverent song,—

" Far, far above thy thought
    His counsel shall appear,
When fully he the work hath wrought
    That caused thy needless fear."

GOD, A MIGHTY FORTRESS.

God is our refuge and strength, a very present help in trouble.— Psalm xlvi., 1.

MARTIN LUTHER

FORTRESS. 8, 7, 6.   Martin Luther.

A mighty fortress is our God,
  A bulwark never failing;
Our helper he amid the flood
  Of mortal ills prevailing.
For still our ancient foe
Doth seek to work us woe;
His craft and power are great;
And, armed with cruel hate,
  On earth is not his equal.

Did we in our own strength confide,
  Our striving would be losing;

Were not the right man on our side,—
  The man of God's own choosing.
Dost ask who that may be?
Christ Jesus: it is he;
Lord Sabaoth his name,
From age to age the same,
  And he must win the battle.

And though this world, with devils filled,
  Should threaten to undo us,
We will not fear; for God hath willed
  His truth to triumph through us.
The Prince of darkness grim,—
We tremble not for him:
His rage we can endure
For, lo! his doom is sure:
  One little word shall fell him.

That word above all earthly powers—
  No thanks to them—abideth;
The spirit and the gift are ours,
  Through him who with us sideth.
Let goods and kindred go,
This mortal life also:
The body they may kill,
God's truth abideth still;
  His kingdom is forever.

—*Martin Luther.*
(Translated by F. H. Hedge.)

116

This hymn should be very near to the heart of every Protestant Christian, for it was written in the year when the Evangelical Princes delivered their historic protest at the Diet of Spires, out of which the word "Protestant," in its present religious sense, was born.   In 1530, while the Diet of Augsburg was in session, Luther used often to sing it to comfort himself and his friends.   It has been called the " Marseillaise of the Reformation."

Born, as this hymn was, in time of storm, it has graced many a stormy scene, not only in Germany, but in other lands.   When the struggle for Protestantism was transferred to the hands of the great king, Gustavus Adolphus, that heroic Swede found comfort and inspiration in Luther's immortal hymn, and commanded it to be sung on the day of his death, at the battlefield of Lutzen.   On the morning of his last battle, when the armies of Gustavus and Wallenstein were drawn up, waiting till the morning mist dispersed to commence the attack, the king commanded this hymn to be sung, accompanied by the drums and trumpets of the whole army.   Immediately afterwards, the mist broke, and the sunshine burst on the two armies.   For a moment Gustavus Adolphus knelt beside his horse, in face of his soldiers, and repeated his usual battle prayer: " O Lord Jesus Christ! bless our arms, and this day's battle, for the glory of thy holy name!"   Then passing along the lines, with a few brief words of encouragement, he gave the battle cry, "God with us!"—the same with which he had conquered at Leipzig. Thus began the day which laid him low amidst the thickest of the fight, with those three sentences on his dying lips, noble and Christian as any that ever fell from the lips of dying man since the days of the last martyr: "I seal with my blood the liberty and religion of the German nation!" "My God, my God!"—and the last that were heard, "Alas! my poor queen!"

Luther's splendid hymn has received many a baptism of fire like that. It is related that on the Sabbath afternoon before the overthrow of the French army in the last Franco-Prussian war, the second Napoleon, then in the shadow of his swiftly-coming doom, rode out to review his troops. In doing so he came near enough to the German camps to hear them singing, and he inquired what it was they sang. He was informed that it was Luther's hymn,—

"A mighty fortress is our God."

It is said that the fated emperor went away sadly, remarking that it was impossible to fight against soldiers who went into battle with hymns like that upon their lips.

This hymn is suggestive of the source of Martin Luther's invincible courage and strength. To him God was ever present, as the source of all blessing. At one time, looking out from his window, he saw a little bird which had just alighted on the bough

"The Prince of darkness grim,—
We tremble not for him"

of a pear tree that grew in his garden. Luther looked upon it and said: "That little bird, how it covers its head with its wings, and will sleep there, so still and fearless, though over it are the infinite starry spaces and the great blue depths of immensity. Yet it fears not: it is at home. The God that made it, too, is there."

Once on coming home from Leipzig in the autumn season, he burst forth in loving wonder at the fields of corn. "How it stands there," he says, "erect on its beautiful taper stem, and bending its beautiful golden head with bread in it—the bread of man sent to him another year."

Thomas Carlyle, who could be bitter enough in his criticism where there was the least shadow of lack of genuineness in a man or his utterances, quotes these passages of Luther's and says: "Such thoughts as these are as little windows through which we gaze into the interior of the depths of Martin Luther's soul, and see visible, across its tempests and clouds, a whole heaven of light and love. He might have painted, he might have sung; could have been beautiful like Raphael, great like Michael Angelo."

The first line of this national hymn of Protestant Germany is very fittingly inscribed on the tomb of the great reformer at Wittenberg, and has been read with tearful eyes by many a Protestant pilgrim to that historic spot.

NEARER HOME.

At evening time it shall be light.—Zachariah xiv., 7.

PHŒBE CARY

CARY. 6. (Irregular.)

Eben Tourjée, Ad. by L. Franklin Snow.

One sweetly solemn thought
   Comes to me o'er and o'er,
I am nearer home to-day,
   Than I ever have been before.

Nearer my Father's house,
   Where the many mansions be,
Nearer the great white throne,
   Nearer the crystal sea.

Nearer the bound of life,
   Where we lay our burdens down,
Nearer leaving the cross,
   Nearer gaining the crown.

But lying darkly between,
   Winding down through shades of night,
Is the silent unknown stream,
   That leads at last to the light.

Closer and closer my steps
  Come to the dread abysm,
Closer death to my lips
  Presses the awful chrism.

Oh, if my mortal feet,
  Have almost gained the brink,
If it be that I'm nearer home,
  Even to-day than I think,

Father, perfect my trust,
  Let my spirit feel in death
That her feet are firmly set
  On the rock of living faith.

— *Phœbe Cary.*

Phœbe Cary wrote this beautiful lyric, which will probably outlive all her other poems, when she was only a girl, seventeen years of age. It was on the Sabbath. She had attended church in the morning, and on coming home to a friend's house, her heart stirred with emotion by the services in which she had but just taken part, she retired to her room and wrote this hymn. Metrical versions have been made by many compilers, and the poem is now found in nearly all the hymn books of the English tongue.

After both she and her hymn had become famous, this friend wrote to her, inquiring about the hymn and its story. In answering her friend's letter she

"I am nearer home to-day,
Than I ever have been before."

says: " I enclose the hymn for you. It was written eighteen years ago (1842) in your own house. I composed it in the little back third-story bedroom, one Sunday morning, after coming from church; and it makes me very happy to think that any word I could say has done any good in the world."

Dr. Russell H. Conwell, of Philadelphia, relates a very beautiful and interesting incident connected with the singing of this hymn. Dr. Conwell was traveling in China and had occasion one day to enter a gambling house in a Chinese city. Among those present were two Americans, one a young man and the other older. They were betting and drinking in a terrible way, the elder one giving utterance continually to the foulest profanity. Two games had been finished, the young man losing each time. The third game, with fresh bottles of liquor, had just begun, and the young man sat lazily back in his chair while his companion shuffled the cards. The man was a long time dealing the cards, and the young man, looking carelessly about the room, began to hum a tune and finally to sing, in a low tone and quite unconsciously, this hymn,—

" One sweetly solemn thought
Comes to me o'er and o'er,
I am nearer home to-day,
Than I ever have been before."

But while the young man sang, his more mature

and more depraved companion stopped dealing the cards, stared at the singer a moment, and then, throwing the cards on the floor, exclaimed,—

"Harry, where did you learn that tune?"

"What tune?"

"Why, the one you have been singing."

The young man said he did not know what he had been singing.

The other repeated the words, with tears in his eyes, and the younger man said he had learned them in a Sunday-school in America.

"Come," said the elder gambler, getting up; "come, Harry; here's what I have won from you; go and use it for some good purpose. As for me, as God sees me, I have played my last game and drank my last bottle. I have misled you, Harry, and I am sorry. Give me your hand, my boy, and say that for old America's sake, if for no other, you will quit this infernal business."

This story gave the greatest happiness to Miss Cary when she heard it. After her death, Dr. Conwell received a letter from the older man referred to in the story, in which he declared that he had become a "hard-working Christian," and that "Harry" had utterly renounced gambling and kindred vices.

Miss Cary did not set a very high value upon this poem when it was written, and was surprised in later years to find that it outran in popularity other poems to whose composition she had given much more thought and time. It doubtless owes its universal success to the fact that it was born out of her own heart experience, and because of that has touched the hearts of readers everywhere.

Phœbe Cary died at the age of forty-seven, and found at the last that the prayer of the closing verse of her hymn was answered,—

> " Father, perfect my trust,
>   Let my spirit feel in death
> That her feet are firmly set
>   On the rock of living faith."

Strangers and pilgrims on the earth. — Hebrews xi., 13.

GANGES. C, P, M.   S. CHANDLER.

How happy is the pilgrim's lot,
How free from every anxious thought,
From worldly hope and fear!
Confined to neither court nor cell,
His soul disdains on earth to dwell —
He only sojourns here.

His happiness in part is mine,
Already saved from self-design,
From every creature-love!
Bless'd with the scorn of finite good,
My soul is lighten'd of its load,
And seeks the things above.

The things eternal I pursue,
A happiness beyond the view
　　Of those that basely pant
For things by nature felt and seen;
Their honors, wealth, and pleasures mean
　　I neither have, nor want.

I have no sharer of my heart,
To rob my Saviour of a part,
　　And desecrate the whole;
Only betroth'd to Christ am I,
And wait his coming from the sky
　　To wed my happy soul.

I have no babes to hold me here,
But children more securely dear
　　For mine I humbly claim;
Better than daughters, or than sons,
Temples divine of living stones,
　　Inscrib'd with Jesus' name.

No foot of land do I possess,
No cottage in this wilderness —
　　A poor wayfaring man;
I lodge awhile in tents below,
Or gladly wander to and fro,
　　Till I my *Canaan* gain.

Nothing on earth I call my own —
A stranger, to the world unknown,
　　I all their goods despise:

I trample on their whole delight,
And seek a country out of sight,
   A country in the skies.

There is my house and portion fair,
My treasure and my heart is there,
   And my abiding home:
For me my elder brethren stay,
And angels beckon me away,
   And Jesus bids me come.

I come; thy servant, Lord, replies;
I come to meet thee in the skies,
   And claim my heavenly rest;
Now let the pilgrim's journey end,
Now, O my Saviour, Brother, Friend,
   Receive me to thy breast.
      —*John Wesley.*

This hymn was written by John Wesley before his marriage, and at a time when it was his determination never to marry. He would have been a far happier man if he had held steadfastly to this determination, for, keen-sighted as he was in his judgment of men, and great as was his executive ability, he was a poor judge of women, and his marriage was the most unhappy feature of his remarkably successful life. His single estate, and the fact that he had given over his property to a board of trustees for benevolent objects, is brought out clearly in the verses,—

" I have no sharer of my heart,
    To rob my Saviour of a part,
        And desecrate the whole;
Only betroth'd to Christ am I,
And wait his coming from the sky
        To wed my happy soul.

" I have no babes to hold me here,
But children more securely dear
        For mine I humbly claim;
Better than daughters, or than sons,
Temples divine of living stones,
        Inscrib'd with Jesus' name.

" No foot of land do I possess,
No cottage in this wilderness —
        A poor wayfaring man;
I lodge awhile in tents below,
Or gladly wander to and fro,
        Till I my *Canaan* gain."

This whole hymn on " The Pilgrim's Lot " was
written out of John Wesley's personal experience.
John Nelson gives us a leaf out of some of the daily
experiences of the leader of the great Methodist revival. He writes: " All that time Mr. Wesley and
I lay on the floor; he had my great-coat for his pil-
low, and I had Burkett's *Notes on the New Testa-
ment* for mine. After being here near three weeks,
one morning about three o'clock, Mr. Wesley turned

"*For me my elder brethren stay,*
And angels beckon me away"

over, and finding me awake, clapped me on the side, saying, ' Brother Nelson, let us be of good cheer; I have one whole side yet, for the skin is off but one side.' We usually preached on the commons, going from one common to another, and it was but seldom any one asked us to eat or drink. One day we had been at St. Hilary Downs, and Mr. Wesley had preached from Ezekiel's vision of dry bones, and there was a shaking among the people as he preached. As we returned, Mr. Wesley stopped his horse to pick the blackberries, saying, ' Brother Nelson, we ought to be thankful that there are plenty of blackberries; for this is the best country I ever saw for getting a stomach, but the worst that ever I saw for getting food.' "

A great many years after this incident, an old Methodist preacher preached in the village on the heights above Marazion, in Cornwall, near St. Hilary Downs. After the service, he was invited to dine with a member of the congregation. The table was somewhat richly laden. For a minute or two he seemed to hesitate in his chair, and at length said:

" Isn't this the place where John Wesley sat in the saddle and dined on blackberries from the hedge for want of a better dinner? "

" Yes," it was replied

" Then," said he, " forbid that I should indulge in this plenty, or eat or drink in this place. Where

Wesley had not a morsel of bread offered him, I will not feast. In honor of his memory I will go down on the downs and fast and pray."

The stalwart old pilgrim stalked away, singing,—

> " His happiness in part is mine,
>   Already saved from self-design,
>   From every creature-love!
> Bless'd with the scorn of finite good,
> My soul is lighten'd of its load,
>   And seeks the things above."

One of the old circuit riders, traveling in the backwoods in the early settlement of Indiana, was enduring, with his family, the deepest poverty. A settler who loved him, being a large landholder, presented him with a title deed of a fertile tract of land. He went home glad at heart, in freedom, as he thought, from his difficulties. Three months after this he came to his friend, the kind-hearted settler. He was welcomed; but he soon drew out the parchment.

" Here, sir," said he, " I want to give you back your title deed."

" What's the matter?" said the other; " any flaw in it?"

" No."

" Isn't it good land?"

" Good as any in the State."

" Do you think I repent the gift?"

"I have not the slightest reason to doubt your generosity."

"Why don't you keep it, then?"

"Well, sir," said the circuit rider, "you know I am very fond of singing, and there is one hymn in my book, the singing of which is one of the greatest comforts of my life. I have not been able to sing it with my whole heart since I have been here. A part of it runs this way,—

> ' No foot of land do I possess,
>   No cottage in this wilderness —
>   A poor wayfaring man;
>   I lodge awhile in tents below,
>   Or gladly wander to and fro,
>   Till I my *Canaan* gain.
>
> ' There is my house and portion fair,
>   My treasure and my heart is there,
>   And my abiding home.' "

"Take your title deed," he added; "I would rather sing that hymn than own America."

He went on his way singing his hymn, and has long since gone to his "abiding home."

THE PILGRIM'S GUIDE.

He leadeth me beside the still waters. — Psalm xxiii., 2.

WILLIAM WILLIAMS

ZION. 8, 7, 4.   Thomas Hastings.

Guide me, O thou great Jehovah,
　　Pilgrim through this barren land;
I am weak, but thou art mighty,
　　Hold me by thy powerful hand;
　　　Bread of heaven,
　　Feed me till I want no more.

Open now the crystal fountain,
　　Whence the healing streams do flow;
Let the fiery cloudy pillar
　　Guide me all my journey through;
　　　Strong Deliverer,
　　Be thou still my strength and shield.

When I tread the verge of Jordan,
　　Bid my anxious fears subside;
Death of death, and hell's destruction,
　　Land me safe on Canaan's side:

Songs of praises
I will ever give to thee.

Musing on my habitation,
Musing on my heavenly home,
Fills my heart with holy longing;
Come, Lord Jesus, quickly come.
Vanity is all I see,
Lord, I long to be with thee.

—*William Williams.*

William Williams was the great hymn-writer of Wales. On account of the variety and uniform excellence of his hymns, he has been styled the "Watts" of his native land. Others have called him "the last lyric poet of South Wales," having reference to the fact that the utterances of his poems and hymns were among the last pure specimens of native Welsh song. Williams was brought up in troublous times. His father was the deacon of an Independent Chapel whose congregation often had to hide in a cave for fear of their persecutors. One Sunday morning the future poet and hymn-writer, as he passed through a little village, heard the church bells ringing and went into the church. The service was dull and uninteresting, and he came out disgusted; but as he came into the open air he saw that the people were standing about waiting for something, and very soon a tall, dark-looking

"Open now the crystal fountain,
Whence the healing streams do flow."

man stood up on one of the gravestones and began to preach. It was the great Whitefield, whose sermons were firing the hearts of the Welsh throughout all their borders. Williams was so much impressed by what he heard that his whole life was altered and he became not only a great hymn-writer but an eloquent preacher as well.

His masterpiece, "Guide me, O thou great Jehovah," like all his hymns, was born out of the heart of Welsh life, and is picturesque with many a reference to rocks and mountains, valleys and brooks, storm and sunshine, wanderings on dangerous narrow paths, and indeed, of wild Welsh nature in all her many moods.

Rev. S. W. Christophers tells a very beautiful story connected with this sweetest of all the minstrelsy of Wales. It was on a summer afternoon in the country, when everything felt quiet and cool after a refreshing shower. In a retired villa a few miles out of London, amidst fruit trees, roses, honeysuckles, and jasmine, there was a summer-like drawing-room looking out, on one side, upon a lawn bounded by stately trees and fringed with flowers, and on the other opening into a little paradise of a conservatory. There in a small elbow-chair sat a dear old woman, a pattern of antique simplicity and gracefulness.

The old lady was dressed in a black silk gown, open at the neck so as to show a snowy neckerchief folded and pinned under the chin; with a small, neatly fringed, cream-colored shawl brought over the shoulders, and fastened at the waist in front, with its corners falling over a white muslin apron. She wore a dainty cap with a modest crown and a neat close border, yet not so close as to hide a clear, open brow, beautiful still; and it seemed more sweetly beautiful with its silvered locks than when it had been richly adorned in the prime of womanhood. The charming old saint's face inspired loving veneration. Her eyes revealed a spiritual depth of kindness and peace. Her features combined to express power, intelligence, gentleness, repose, and love. And there was something in the expression which inspired the thought of a transition already begun between mortal age and immortal youth. In opinion, taste, and feeling she was an amiable representative of the last century; used to close and acute observation, well-informed, remarkable for good sense, with a tenacious memory and pleasant command of her native English, she was one of those rarely beautiful old people who can really help a later generation to realize the life of older times.

This dear old saint, after a conversation with her friend, seemed for a while to be musing, and then, whispering in reply to her friend's question, she said, "It was as if He talked with me." And when, a little later, she sat murmuring a song in

sweet undertones, it was asked, "What are you singing? Shall I join you?"

"I was singing," said she,—

> "When I tread the verge of Jordan,
>   Bid my anxious fears subside;
> Death of death, and hell's destruction,
>   Land me safe on Canaan's side:
>   Songs of praises
>   I will ever give to thee."

BEFORE THE CROSS.

Looking unto Jesus, the author and finisher of our faith.— Hebrews xii., 2.

RAY PALMER

OLIVET. 8, 4.   LOWELL MASON.

My faith looks up to thee,
Thou Lamb of Calvary,
   Savior divine!
Now hear me while I pray:
Take all my guilt away;
O let me from this day
   Be wholly thine!

May thy rich grace impart
Strength to my fainting heart,
   My zeal inspire!
As thou hast died for me,
Oh, may my love to thee
Pure, warm, and changeless be,
   A living fire!

While life's dark maze I tread,
And griefs around me spread,
   Be thou my guide!

Bid darkness turn to day,
Wipe sorrow's tears away,
Nor let me ever stray
From thee aside.

When ends life's transient dream,
When death's cold, sullen stream
Shall o'er me roll,
Blest Savior, then in love
Fear and distrust remove!
O bear me safe above,
A ransomed soul!

—*Ray Palmer.*

This is, without doubt, the most spiritual of all
American hymns. It was written by Dr. Ray Palmer when a very young man, " between his college
and theological studies." The hymn was the expression of his own spiritual longing. He was in
very delicate health at the time, and in the discour-
agements of such a condition, his thought turned
toward the Savior as the one hope upon which he
could rest. The Psalmist's declaration concerning
others, that " they looked unto him and were lightened," proved true in his case.

The hymn was written without the slightest idea
of publication, and without the expectation that any
eye other than the author's would look on it. It
was a meditation on spiritual things that the poetic

*"Now let me ever stray
From thee aside."*

mind of Palmer formulated into verse. He says concerning the writing: " I gave form to what I felt, by writing, with little effort, the stanzas. I recollect I wrote them with very tender emotions and ended the last line with tears."

The little slip on which the hymn had been written was carried about in the author's pocketbook for a long time. One day, on the street, he met his friend, Lowell Mason, the well-known musician, and in the course of their conversation Mason inquired of Palmer if he did not have a hymn which he would be willing to contribute to his new book. The young poet opened his pocketbook and produced the little hymn, then two or three years old. Lowell Mason was at once attracted by it and desired a copy. This incident occurred in Boston, and the two friends stepped together into a store, where the copy was made and carried away by the musician. On re-reading the hymn in his study, Mason was so impressed by it that he composed for it the tune of Olivet, which is admirably adapted to the words.

A few days afterwards, when Mason again met Palmer on the street, his first words were: " Mr. Palmer, you may live many years, and do many good things, but I think you will be best known to posterity as the author of ' My Faith Looks up to Thee,' " which prophecy has already been fulfilled.

It is strange that, on first being printed, it received no particular notice. It had, however, been reprinted in a number of religious newspapers, from one of which Dr. Andrew Reed, of Scotland, clipped it while he was traveling in this country. The name of the author was not given, and Dr. Reed took it up as a waif and inserted it in a new hymn book which he was preparing, publishing it anonymously. It thus came to be well known abroad before it began to receive recognition here. It has long since, however, conquered all indifference, is in all the hymnals, and is a universal favorite.

Dr. Duffield, in his *English Hymns*, tells the story of Mrs. Layyah Barakat, a native Syrian woman who was educated in the schools at Beirut and afterward married and went as a teacher to Egypt. Years later, when exiled for a time, she traveled in this country, and among other incidents she related that she had been permitted to see the conversion of her whole family, who were Maronites of Mount Lebanon. Her mother, then sixty-two years of age, was taught by her this hymn in Arabic. They would sit on the house roof and repeat it together; and when the news came back to Syria that the daughter was safe in America, the mother could send her no better proof of her faith and love than in the trustful words of this precious hymn, assuring her that her faith still looked up to the Lamb of Calvary.

Among many helpful incidents connected with this hymn of the heart, none are more touching

than this: On the eve of one of the most fearful
battles of our Civil War, a group of young soldiers
had assembled in a tent for prayer. They knew
quite well they might die in the battle, and if such
should be their fate, they wished their friends to
know that they had died in the faith of Christ; so
one of them wrote out this hymn, and each man
signed his name at the bottom of the paper. Only
one survived the battle, and he told the story.

THE STAR OF BETHLEHEM.

When they saw the star, they rejoiced with exceeding great joy. — Matthew ii., 10.

HENRY KIRKE WHITE

MISSIONARY CHANT. L. M.

HEINRICH CHRISTOPHER ZEUNER.

When marshalled on the nightly plain,
   The glittering host bestud the sky,
One star alone of all the train
   Can fix the sinner's wandering eye.

Hark! hark! to God the chorus breaks,
   From every host, from every gem;
But one alone the Saviour speaks,
   It is the Star of Bethlehem.

Once on the raging seas I rode,
   The storm was loud, the night was dark,
The ocean yawned, and rudely blowed
   The wind that tossed my foundering bark.

Deep horror then my vitals froze;
   Death-struck, I ceased the tide to stem;
When suddenly a star arose,
   It was the Star of Bethlehem.

It was my guide, my light, my all,
　　It bade my dark forebodings cease;
And, through the storm and danger s thrall,
　　It led me to the port of peace.

Now safely moored, my perils o'er,
　　I'll sing, first in night's diadem,
Forever and forever more,
　　The Star, the Star of Bethlehem.

　　　　　　　　—*Henry Kirke White.*

Henry Kirke White died when he was but twenty
years of age, yet notwithstanding this fact, and the
added one that he was born to the humblest circumstances in life, the poet Southey gladly became his
enthusiastic biographer, and the aristocratic Byron
was his brilliant eulogist. He wrote but ten hymns;
he needed to write only this one to earn immortality
in the memories and hearts of all lovers of sacred
song.

The circumstances connected with the writing of
this hymn are of the greatest interest: During his
school days White was a skeptic, and, with the giddy
recklessness of youth, was accustomed to scoff at
and ridicule religious things. His most intimate
friend in school was a young man named Almond,
who, though not a Christian, had an inquiring and
serious mind which was open to evidence on the
subject of Christianity.

On one occasion Almond was called to the bedside

of another friend who was a believer in Christ, and who met death with great peace and comfort. The triumphs of faith which he then witnessed greatly impressed the youth, and fully convinced him of the truth of religion and determined him to become a Christian. Being of rather a timid disposition, he hesitated to make known his change of mind and feeling to White for fear of the shafts of ridicule which he supposed his friend would hurl against him.

He endeavored for a time to continue his friendship with White, while in secret he sought communion with the Savior. Finding that this manner of life brought him no peace, he finally determined to give up the society of his friend and openly avow himself a believer in Christ.

The young poet felt the neglect of his friend very keenly, and sought him out and inquired the cause of his change of manner. Almond, thus confronted, frankly confessed the complete transformation that had taken place in his convictions, and declared his resolution to lead a Christian life. This conduct seemed to White to imply that he was an unworthy companion for any one who was seeking to live the life of a Christian, and his sensitive nature was deeply hurt.

" Good God, Almond! " he exclaimed, " you surely regard me in a worse light than I deserve."

The change that had come over Almond so deeply

impressed White that his skeptical views were shaken. He began to study into the matter more earnestly, and was ere long convinced of the divinity of Christ and sought him as his personal Savior. The two young men then renewed their friendship, which became more intimate and beautiful than ever, glorified by this new and higher sympathy.

It is this personal experience which White relates with such graphic portraiture in his great hymn. If we read some of these verses again, putting this personal element into them, we shall see how clearly and strongly he tells the story of his soul's conversion,—

" Once on the raging seas I rode,
    The storm was loud, the night was dark,
The ocean yawned, and rudely blowed
    The wind that tossed my foundering bark.

" Deep horror then my vitals froze;
    Death-struck, I ceased the tide to stem;
When suddenly a star arose,
    It was the Star of Bethlehem.

" It was my guide, my light, my all,
    It bade my dark forebodings cease;
And, through the storm and danger's thrall,
    It led me to the port of peace."

White, who had intended before to be an attorney, now determined on entering the ministry; but his

"...And, through the storm and danger's thrall.
It led me to the port of peace"

frail body gave way at the very opening of a promising career. How brilliant that promise must have been one may easily infer from the fact that Lord Byron, from amidst the bitter satire and cruel invective of his *English Bards and Scotch Reviewers*, pauses with gentle tearfulness to lay a beautiful wreath on the grave of this noble youth. Happy for Byron's pen if it had always been as well guided as in celebrating this event: —

" Unhappy White! When life was in its spring,
And thy young muse just waved her joyous wing,
The spoiler swept that soaring lyre away,
Which else had sounded an immortal lay!
Oh, what a noble heart was here undone,
When Science' self destroyed her favorite son!

" 'Twas thine own genius gave the final blow,
And helped to plant the wound that laid thee low
So the struck eagle stretched upon the plain,
No more through rolling clouds to soar again, —
Viewed his own feather on the fatal dart,
And winged the shaft that quivered to his heart."

But Byron was mistaken, brief as Henry Kirke White's life had been, his muse had already "sounded an immortal lay" in this beautiful hymn, which will go on blessing the world through all time.

PRESSING ON IN THE CHRISTIAN RACE.

I press toward the mark for the prize of the high calling of God in Christ Jesus.— Philippians iii., 14.

CHRISTMAS. C. M. GEORGE FREDERICK HANDEL.

Awake, my soul, stretch every nerve,
  And press with vigour on;
A heavenly race demands thy zeal,
  And an immortal crown.

A cloud of witnesses around
  Hold thee in full survey;
Forget the steps already trod,
  And onward urge thy way.

'Tis God's all-animating voice
  That calls thee from on high;
'Tis his own hand presents the prize
  To thine aspiring eye —

That prize, with peerless glories bright.
  Which shall new luster boast
When victors' wreaths and monarchs' gems
  Shall blend in common dust.

Blest Saviour, introduced by thee,
    Have I my race begun
And, crowned with victory, at thy feet
    I'll lay my honors down.

—*Philip Doddridge.*

No other hymn-writers save Charles Wesley and Isaac Watts have left so many hymns which are in common use to-day as Philip Doddridge. Doddridge was a tireless literary worker, and left many excellent volumes as the fruits of his pen. The sentiment of his family motto, " *Dum vivimus vivamus,*" was highly eulogized by Johnson in his celebrated lines: —

" ' Live while you live,' the epicure would say,
    ' And seize the pleasures of the present day.'
    ' Live while you live,' the sacred preacher cries,
    ' And give to God each moment as it flies.'
    Lord, in my life let both unite in thee:
    I live in pleasure while I live to thee! "

The hymn we are studying is in the spirit of this motto. Doddridge's hymns were almost always written for immediate use in connection with his sermons. They have been compared to " spiritual amber fetched up and floated off from sermons long since lost in the depths of bygone time." Strange to say, his hymns were not printed during the author's lifetime.

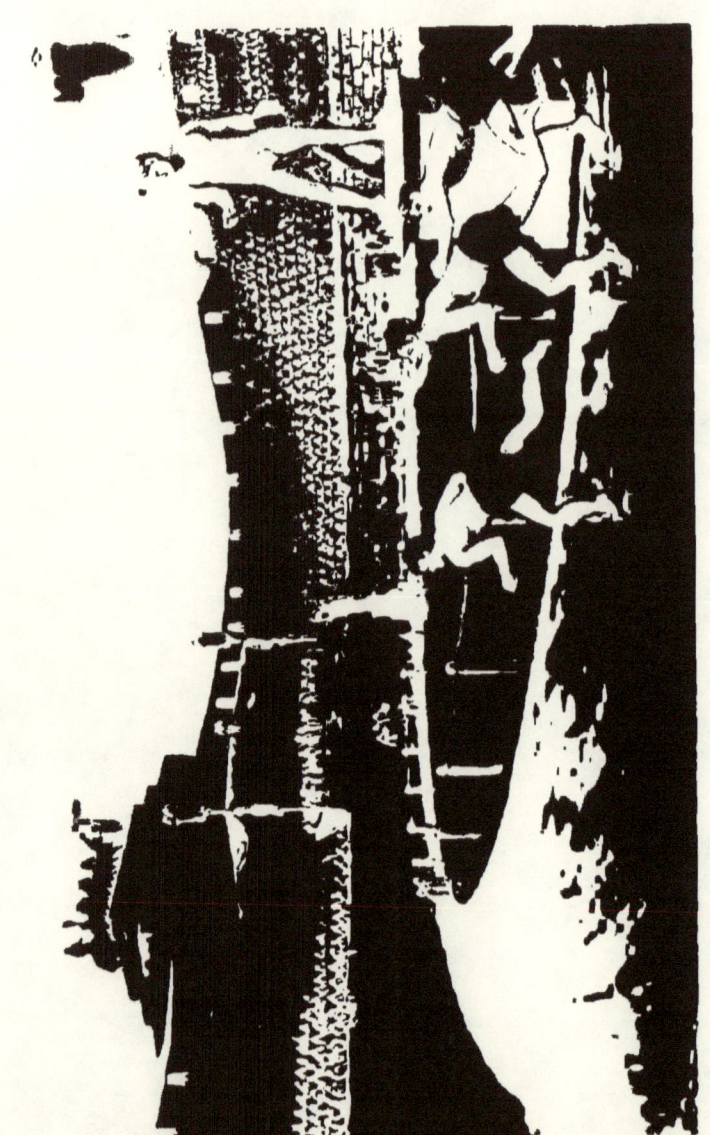

"A cloud of witnesses around
Hold thee in full survey"

Dr. Doddridge often found the theme of his discourses, and the hymns which sprang into being with them, in visions which came to him in sleep. Mr. Harsha, his biographer, relates that on one occasion he retired to sleep after a conversation on the state of the soul after death. In the sleep which followed he dreamed that he was dead, and that his spirit soared away into those deep regions of the infinite which oftentimes awaken our trembling curiosity. He felt, as he lost sight of this noisy, busy world, how vain and empty are the objects which excite its inhabitants so much; and, while musing on the theme, and committing himself to the care of the Divine Pilot as he embarked on the ocean of immensity and sailed amidst islands of stars, he fancied he was met on the shores of heaven by an angel-guide, who conducted him to a palace which had been assigned for his abode.

The dreamer wondered at the place, for it made him think that heaven was not so unlike earth as the teachings of Scripture had led him to expect; but he was told that there he was to be gradually prepared for unknown glories afterwards to be revealed. In the inner apartment of the palace stood a golden cup, with a grape-vine embossed on it, which he learned was meant to signify the living union of Christ and his people. But as he and his guide were talking, a gentle knock at the door before him announced the approach of some one, and the unfolding portals revealed the majestic presence of the Redeemer. The now glorified disciple immediately fell at the feet of his gracious Lord, but was raised with assurances of favor and of the kind acceptance which had been vouchsafed to all his loving services. Then, taking up the cup and drinking out of it, the Savior put it in Dr. Doddridge's hand, inviting him to drink He shrunk from so great an honor, but was told, " If thou drink it not, thou hast no part with me."

He was ready to sink under the transport of gratitude and joy when the Savior, in consideration of his meekness, left him for a while, with the assurance that he would soon return; directing him, in the meantime, to look and meditate upon the objects that were around; and lo! there were pictures hung all about, illustrative of his own pilgrim-life; scene after scene of trial and deliverance, of conflict and victory, meeting his eyes and filling his heart with love and wonder And, as he gazed on them, he thought — what we often fancy will be the saint's first thought in heaven — how all the perils of his former life were over. Exulting in his new-found safety, a burst of joy broke the enchantment of his celestial dream and he awoke again, amidst a flood of tears, to the consciousness that he was in the body still.

No wonder that Doddridge arose from visions like that to write of the glorious realities of the spiritual world in lines that have inspired the church in every land. " The prize " about which he sings was so real to him that he makes it seem real to us, —

> " That prize, with peerless glories bright,
>   Which shall new luster boast
> When victors' wreaths and monarchs' gems
>   Shall blend in common dust."

HYMN TO THE GOD OF ABRAHAM.

I am the Lord God of Abraham. — Genesis xxviii., 13.

"The God of Abraham praise."

LEONI. 6, 8, 4.   AD. BY RABBI LEONI.

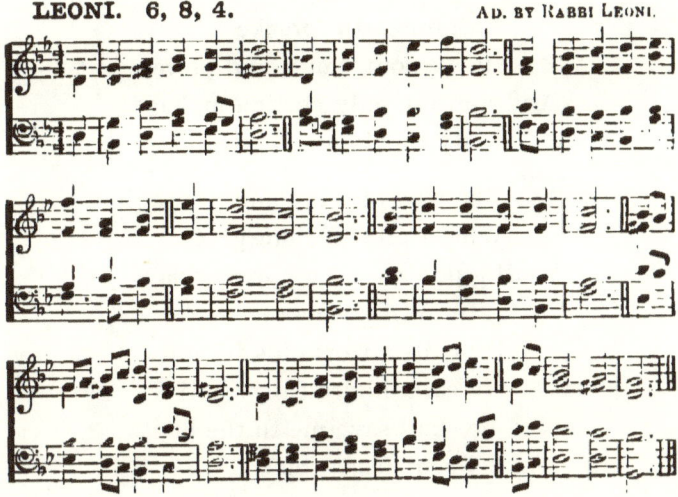

The God of Abraham praise,
Who reigns enthron'd above;
Ancient of everlasting days,
And God of love:
Jehovah — great I AM —
By earth and heaven confess'd;
I bow and bless the sacred name,
Forever bless'd.

The God of Abraham praise,
At whose supreme command,
From earth I rise, and seek the joys
At his right hand:

I all on earth forsake,
Its wisdom, fame, and power;
And him my only portion make,
My Shield and Tower.

The God of Abraham praise,
Whose all-sufficient grace
Shall guide me all my happy days,
In all my ways:
He calls a worm his friend!
He calls himself my God!
And he shall save me to the end,
Thro' Jesus' blood.

He by himself hath sworn!
I on his oath depend,
I shall, on eagle's wings upborne,
To heaven ascend;
I shall behold his face,
I shall his power adore,
And sing the wonders of his grace
For evermore.

Tho' nature's strength decay,
And earth and hell withstand,
To Canaan's bounds I urge my way
At his command:
The wat'ry deep I pass,
With Jesus in my view;
And thro' the howling wilderness
My way pursue.

The goodly land I see,
With peace and plenty bless'd;
A land of sacred liberty
And endless rest.
There milk and honey flow,
And oil and wine abound,
And trees of life forever grow,
With mercy crown'd.

There dwells the Lord our King,
The Lord our Righteousness,
Triumphant o'er the world and sin,
The Prince of Peace:
On Sion's sacred heights
His kingdom still maintains;
And glorious, with his saints in light
Forever reigns.

He keeps his own secure,
He guards them by his side,
Arrays in garments white and pure
His spotless bride.
With streams of sacred bliss,
With groves of living joys,
With all the fruits of Paradise
He still supplies.

Before the great Three-One
They all exulting stand;
And tell the wonders he hath done,
Thro' all their land:

The listening spheres attend,
And swell the growing fame;
And sing in songs which never end,
The wondrous Name.

The God who reigns on high,
The great archangels sing,
And " Holy, holy, holy," cry,
" Almighty King!
Who was, and is, the same!
And evermore shall be;
Jehovah — Father — Great I AM!
We worship thee."

Before the Saviour's face
The ransom'd nations bow;
O'erwhelm'd at his almighty grace,
Forever new:
He shows his prints of love,—
They kindle to a flame!
And sound through all the worlds above,
The slaughter'd Lamb.

The whole triumphant host
Give thanks to God on high;
" Hail, Father, Son, and Holy Ghost!"
They ever cry:
Hail, Abraham's God — and *mine!*
I join the heavenly lays,
All might and majesty are thine,
And endless praise.
          —*Thomas Olivers.*

So fine a hymn-writer and so rare a critic of devotional poetry as James Montgomery, writing of this hymn, says: " There is not in our language a lyric of more majestic style, more elevated thought or more glorious imagery; its structure, indeed, is unattractive; and, on account of the short lines, occasionally uncouth; but, like a stately pile of architecture, severe and simple in design, it strikes less on the first view than after deliberate examination, when its proportions become more graceful, its dimensions expand, and the mind itself grows greater in contemplating it. The man who wrote this hymn must have had the finest ear imaginable; for on account of the peculiarity of the measure, none but a person of equal musical and poetic tastes could have produced the harmony perceptible in the verse."

Olivers conceived this hymn while visiting a Jewish synagogue in company with his friend, John Bakewell, himself a hymn-writer of a high order. During the service in the synagogue, Olivers was so deeply impressed with an old Hebrew melody sung by Dr. Leoni that he could scarcely wait till his return home to write out the hymn that was surging in his brain, and which he metrically adapted to the same splendid tune.

Olivers lived to see the issue of at least thirty editions of this hymn. It has been ever a hymn fruitful in comfort to worshipful souls, especially to those in trial, or conscious of the near approach of death. It may be doubted whether any other hymn has been more frequently on the lips of dying saints.

The wife of the celebrated William Carvosso, a woman of beautiful character, was called for the last eighteen months of her life to endure extreme suffering. During all this time, however, her cheerful face was a comfort to all who saw her, and scarce a day passed that she did not sing with joyous hope some portion of Olivers' hymn. Now it would be, —

> " The God of Abraham praise,
> At whose supreme command,
> From earth I rise, and seek the joys
> At his right hand:
> I all on earth forsake,
> Its wisdom, fame, and power;
> And him my only portion make,
> My Shield and Tower."

And then frequently, —

> " He by himself hath sworn!
> I on his oath depend,
> I shall, on eagle's wings upborne,
> To heaven ascend."

Thus resting her soul on the Divine oath, she passed rejoicing into heaven.

In a snug little retreat under a hillside, near Cal-

lington, in the West of England, the early preachers of the Wesleyan reformation used to be entertained, with motherly affection, by a Mrs. Geake, a
woman of remarkable spiritual cultivation. When
the good woman was young, she was always ready,
in the warmth of her zeal, to go from place to place,
assisting the preachers by the use of her fine voice
in singing. And now, when beyond eighty, she
would say, " My voice is weak, but I can sing still,
my heart sings; and often of an evening I lift up
my song."

"Can't you give me a morning song?" said a
friend one day, a little while before she passed over
to her reward. " Yes, I think I can." And then,
in a thin, tremulous tone, she sang from her favorite
hymn, which she said Dr. Adam Clarke had taught
her while she was a girl, when he used to preach in
her father's parlor. These were the triumphant
verses, —

" Tho' nature's strength decay,
And earth and hell withstand,
To Canaan's bounds I urge my way
At his command;
The wat'ry deep I pass,
With Jesus in my view;
And thro' the howling wilderness
My way pursue.

" The goodly land I see,
    With peace and plenty bless'd,
A land of sacred liberty
    And endless rest.
There milk and honey flow,
    And oil and wine abound,
And trees of life forever grow,
    With mercy crown'd."

Rev. William Worth, noted for the saintliness of his personal character, was nearing the end of his earthly pilgrimage. He had been lying for some time in silence, with an air as though he were listening attentively. At length he said: "Hark! do you hear that sweet music? Yes," he added, speaking to the unseen, "precious Savior, thou art mine!" Then, breaking forth into praise he exclaimed,—

" I shall behold his face,
    I shall his power adore,
And sing the wonders of his grace
    For evermore!"

And so, with glorious visions entranced, he passed up to " behold his face," for evermore.

BROTHERLY LOVE.

Let brotherly love continue. — Hebrews xiii., 1.

JOHN FAWCETT

DENNIS. S. M. HANS GEORGE NAEGELI.

Blest be the tie that binds
  Our hearts in Christian love;
The fellowship of kindred minds
  Is like to that above.

Before our Father's throne,
  We pour our ardent prayers;
Our fears, our hopes, our aims are one,
  Our comforts and our cares.

We share our mutual woes,
  Our mutual burdens bear;
And often for each other flows
  The sympathizing tear.

When we asunder part,
  It gives us inward pain;
But we shall still be joined in heart,
  And hope to meet again.

213

This glorious hope revives
 Our courage by the way;
While each in expectation lives,
 And longs to see the day.

From sorrow, toil, and pain,
 And sin we shall be free;
And perfect love and friendship reign
 Through all eternity.

—John Fawcett.

This, the sweetest of all the hymns that voice the joys of Christian brotherhood, was inspired by an incident as touching and tender as the hymn itself. Dr. Fawcett had been preaching for a number of years to a faithful and loving flock near Wainsgate, in Yorkshire, England. His family had increased and the small income the church at that place was able to pay him had remained stationary, so he thought it was his duty to accept a call which he had received to become the pastor of a church in London. He preached his farewell sermon to his church in Yorkshire, and loaded six or seven wagons with his library and his household goods, preparatory to making the journey to his new home. At last, the family were all ready for departure; but meanwhile the members of his poor church were almost broken-hearted, and men, women, and children gathered about them, in tears, and be-

"When we asunder part,
It gives us inward pain"

sought him, even then, not to leave them. Dr. Fawcett and his wife, overcome with emotion, sat down side by side on one of the packing cases and wept bitterly.

Looking up, Mrs. Fawcett said, in a voice choking with emotion, " O John, John, I cannot bear this! I know not how to go! "

" Nor I, either," said the gentle-souled preacher. " Nor will we go. Unload the wagons, and put everything in the place where it was before."

The people of Wainsgate cried for joy, and hastened to get the furniture and books back into the house again. A letter was sent to the church in London to explain to them why his coming was impossible; and the big-hearted pastor renewed his labors on a salary of less than two hundred dollars a year. This famous hymn was written to commemorate this event.

There are many tender and loving associations connected with this song of the heart. Mr. D. L. Moody relates that in his early experience as a Sunday-school superintendent in Chicago he had a class of girls whom he gave into the charge of a teacher, a gentleman who, as he thought, would be able to interest them and keep them quiet. It was before the days of Mr. Moody's baptism of evangelistic fire, and when he did not press the matter of personal religion so much as now. One day this teacher came to Mr. Moody quite disheartened and sad.

He had had a severe attack of hemorrhage of the
lungs, and his physician had ordered him away from
Chicago to a milder climate. He feared that he
was nearing the end of his life, and felt greatly
condemned that he had made no true effort to save
the souls of his class. His evident despair and bitter remorse over failure to do his duty aroused Mr.
Moody to propose that they should go together and
visit each of the young ladies. They took a car-
riage, and began their work, the teacher, though
very feeble, conversing with each one as best he
could. They continued this direct and faithful
effort for ten days, and by that time every one had
yielded her heart to Christ; and when at length this
was accomplished, they were all gathered for a farewell meeting at the teacher's house, and there they
began to sing this hymn,—

> " Blest be the tie that binds
> Our hearts in Christian love;
> The fellowship of kindred minds
> Is like to that above."

But when they reached the verse,—

> " When we asunder part,"

their hearts were too full, and their voices failed.
The great evangelist declares that it was the most
affecting meeting he ever attended.

The next day the teacher was to depart for his

new home, and every member of his class, with the
superintendent, gathered at the railway station to
bid him a final good-bye. The faithful teacher,
happy in the thought of the glorious success which
had been given him at the last, stood on the plat-
form of the car, pointing upward as the train moved
away, thus indicating the closing verses of the
hymn their tears would not permit them to sing,—

> " This glorious hope revives
>   Our courage by the way;
>   While each in expectation lives,
>   And longs to see the day

> " From sorrow, toil, and pain,
>   And sin we shall be free;
>   And perfect love and friendship reign
>   Through all eternity."

LAMB OF GOD.

Him that cometh to me I will in no wise cast out.
—John vi., 37.

CHARLOTTE ELLIOTT

WOODWORTH. L. M.   WILLIAM BATCHELDER BRADBURY.

Just as I am, without one plea,
But that thy blood was shed for me,
And that thou bidd'st me come to thee,
O Lamb of God, I come!

Just as I am, and waiting not,
To rid my soul of one dark blot,
To thee, whose blood can cleanse each spot,
O Lamb of God, I come!

Just as I am, though tossed about
With many a conflict, many a doubt,
Fightings and fears within, without,
O Lamb of God, I come!

Just as I am, poor, wretched, blind,
Sight, riches, healing of the mind,
Yea, all I need, in thee to find,
O Lamb of God, I come!

225

Just as I am, thou wilt receive,
Wilt welcome, pardon, cleanse, relieve!
Because thy promise I believe,
    O Lamb of God, I come!

Just as I am,—thy love unknown
Has broken every barrier down,—
Now, to be thine, yea, thine alone,
    O Lamb of God, I come!

Just as I am, of that free love
The breadth, length, depth, and height to
    prove,
Here for a season, then above,
    O Lamb of God, I come!
               —*Charlotte Elliott.*

Dr. Cæsar Malan, of Geneva, Switzerland, was being entertained in the home of Miss Elliott. The young lady was then in failing health, and during an evening conversation that earnest missionary asked her if she thought herself to be an experimental Christian. She was at first inclined to resent so personal a conversation, and replied that personal religion was a matter she did not wish to discuss. Dr. Malan answered with great gentleness that he would not pursue the matter if it displeased her, but he would pray that she might become a Christian. Some days afterwards she apologized to the minister for her rude answer, and said: " I do not know how to find Christ. I want you to help me."

Dr. Malan's reply was, "Come to him *just as you are.*" Neither of them thought at the time that that simple reply would be caught up in song by the whole Christian world, and be repeated for many years to come.

It was this reply of Dr. Malan to her personal question that first led to her own conversion, which was Miss Elliott's inspiration in writing her famous hymn.

The hymn has been so constantly used and is so greatly loved that there are many incidents telling of comfort received from it.

One Sunday evening in the summer of 1895 Dr. D. W. Couch went into his pulpit in Lenox Road Methodist Church, Brooklyn, prepared to reason with some backsliders who had promised him to be present. It was a warm evening, and raining. The persons he had expected were not in attendance. He lingered as long as he could before opening the service, and knew not what was best to do. He lifted his heart to God, and said, "Help me!" A text that he had used a long time before came to his mind and opened up in a lucid manner. Turning to the leader of the choir he said: "I shall be glad to change the hymns." He replied: "Give us something familiar." The minister arose and announced, "Just as I am, without one plea."

The church windows were open. A young lawyer, the son of a minister, was lying in his room in the second house from the church, the windows of his room open, also. He was listening to every word of the hymn. Dr. Couch did not know at the time that they had sung the same hymn at the young people's meeting, in the room below, a few minutes before.

The next morning the minister received a note from the lawyer, saying, "I desire to see you as early as ten o'clock on Tuesday morning. Do not fail to be here at that time. I believe I have something important to tell you."

At the time appointed Dr. Couch was in his room. The young man reached out his hand, and, with eyes full of tears and a voice choked with emotion, said, "I want to tell you that I have found Jesus Christ to be the Savior of my soul."

He then said, "Let me tell you how it came about. Sunday night I was lying here thinking of the past and the future, reflecting upon my father's teachings and my mother's prayers, and I wished that it were possible for me to be a Christian. But, I thought, I have sinned against too great light; I have resisted the best influences until it is too late. At that moment, in the young people's meeting, they began singing, —

> ' Just as I am, without one plea,
> But that thy blood was shed for me,
> And that thou bidd'st me come to thee,
> O Lamb of God, I come!'

"Just as I am, thou wilt receive,
Will welcome, pardon, cleanse, relieve

and I said, ' Does he bid me come now? No; it cannot be. I remember when he did, but I have resisted influences for good too long. How I wish I might come!' And while struggling with my thoughts, you opened the meeting in the audience room, with, —

> ' Just as I am, without one plea,
> But that thy blood was shed for me,
> And that thou bidd'st me come to thee.'

I said, ' What does that mean? Does he bid me come to him after all? It must be so. That hymn is repeated for me;' and I cried out, ' O Lamb of God, I come. I do come!'

" I had a sleepless night. In the morning he appeared. My room was filled with light, my soul with joy. I knew he saved me, but I thought I would wait until the next day before telling you, that I might be certain that it was not emotion only. But now I know that I am his. Won't my father and mother be glad?"

We can never know how many wandering souls, all around the world, have found that sweet hymn their guiding star to the Mercy Seat; but no doubt Miss Elliott's brother, Rev. H. V. Elliott, was warranted in speaking as he did with reference to this hymn. " In the course of a long ministry, I hope I have been permitted to see some fruit of my labors, but I feel that far more has been done by a single hymn of my sister's."

231

AMERICA.

A pleasant land, a goodly heritage of the hosts of nations. — Jeremiah iii., 19.

SAMUEL FRANCIS SMITH

AMERICA. 6, 4. HENRY CAREY.

My country! 'tis of thee,
Sweet land of liberty,
　Of thee I sing;
Land where my fathers died!
Land of the Pilgrims' pride!
From every mountain-side
　Let freedom ring!

My native country, thee —
Land of the noble, free —
　Thy name I love;
I love thy rocks and rills,
Thy woods and templed hills;
My heart with rapture thrills
　Like that above.

Let music swell the breeze,
And ring from all the trees

237

Sweet freedom's song;
Let mortal tongues awake;
Let all that breathe partake;
Let rocks their silence break —
The sound prolong.

Our fathers' God! to thee,
Author of liberty,
To thee we sing;
Long may our land be bright
With freedom's holy light;
Protect us by thy might,
Great God, our King!
—*Samuel Francis Smith*

There can be no doubt about the destined immortality of this hymn. Although it has never been chosen as a National Hymn by any action of Congress, or proclamation of President, it has been selected by a still greater authority — the people themselves. To the great public, rich or poor, it is and will continue to be the National Hymn so long as American liberty shall last.

At the time of its writing its author was a young theological student in Andover, Massachusetts, having but recently graduated from Harvard, in the same class with the famous poet, Oliver Wendell Holmes. His distinguished classmate, in a well known class poem entitled "The Boys," pays a very neat tribute to the author of "America.—"

"And there's a nice youngster of excellent pith,—
Fate tried to conceal him by naming him Smith,
But he shouted a song for the brave and the free,—
Just read on his medal, ' My country,' ' of thee!' "

To be the author of such a hymn is enough for one
man to carry on his medal.   It was written without
the slightest thought on the part of the author of its
ever becoming a National Hymn.   It was first sung
at a children's Fourth of July celebration in Park √
Street Church, Boston.   The tune, selected for it by
Mr Smith himself, was found by him in a German
music book, which was presented to him by Lowell
Mason, the musician, who remarked on the occasion
of its gift, " You can read German books, and I
cannot."   It is certainly a very remarkable coinci-
dence that he should have selected the same tune
which has been used as the British national tune
since the days of George II.
    This tune has a disputed history.   It is generally
considered to be an amendment made by Henry
Carey, near the close of the seventeenth century, to
a tune composed by Dr. John Bull, who died in
1628.   When the tune was first brought to England,
the publisher, no doubt desiring to gain Royal attention by it, published it in honor of George II.
French critics, however, claim that the original
music was composed by Lulli, and that it was sung
by three hundred young ladies before Louis XIV.,

at Saint Cyr, where Handel found it in 1721. If all these claims are correct, this has been in some sense a national tune in three governments.

No other hymn is used so widely and so constantly in the public schools of the United States. The following anonymous verses which have been widely printed contain an admirable tribute to this voicing of the patriotic devotion of American youth. The verses are entitled "Passing the Primary School."

" Again each morning as we pass
    The city's streets along,
We hear the voices of the class
    Ring out the nation's song.

" The small boys' treble piping clear,
    The bigger boys' low growl,
And from the boy that has no ear
    A weird, discordant howl.

" With swelling hearts we hear them sing
    ' My country, 'tis of thee '—
From childish throats the anthem ring,
    ' Sweet land of liberty!'

" Their little hearts aglow with pride,
    Each with exultant tongue
Proclaims: ' From every mountain-side
    Let Freedom's song be sung '

" Let him who'd criticise the time,
     Or scout the harmony,
  Betake him to some other clime —
     No patriot is he!

" From scenes like these our grandeur springs.
     And we shall e'er be strong,
  While o'er the land the school-house rings
     Each day with Freedom's song."

Once in a far Western city the school board, for the time being, was dominated by a man who was very bigoted in his agnosticism, and bitterly resented anything that smacked of the Bible or worship of God. He refused to permit the teachers to read the Bible, or to teach the children religious hymns. They, being earnest Christians, consoled themselves and in a measure thwarted his unholy purpose by leading their scholars, the first thing in the morning and the last in the evening, in the singing of America. Even the agnostic did not dare prohibit that. The hope of American civilization lies most of all in maintaining in the hearts of the people the love of liberty and reverent confidence in God which breathes and throbs in this noble hymn. Liberty-loving Americans rise to the highest note of patriotism and lofty devotion as they sing,—

" Our fathers' God! to thee,
Author of liberty,
To thee we sing:
Long may our land be bright
With freedom's holy light;
Protect us by thy might,
Great God, our King!"

DESIRING TO PRAISE WORTHILY.

Hitherto hath the Lord helped us.— 1 Samuel vii., 12.

ROBERT ROBINSON

NETTLETON. 8, 7. D.
UNKNOWN.

Come, thou fount of every blessing,
　　Tune my heart to sing thy grace:
Streams of mercy, never ceasing,
　　Call for songs of loudest praise.
Teach me some celestial measure,
　　Sung by ransomed hosts above;
Oh, the vast, the boundless treasure
　　Of my Lord's unchanging love!

Here I raise my Ebenezer;
　　Hither by thy help I'm come;
And I hope, by thy good pleasure,
　　Safely to arrive at home.
Jesus sought me when a stranger,
　　Wandering from the fold of God,
He, to save my soul from danger,
　　Interposed his precious blood.

Oh! to grace how great a debtor
    Daily I'm constrained to be;
Let that grace, Lord, like a fetter,
    Bind my wandering soul to thee.
Prone to wander, Lord, I feel it;
    Prone to leave the God I love;
Here's my heart, Lord, take and seal it,
    Seal it from thy courts above.

Oh, that day when, freed from sinning,
    I shall see thy lovely face;
Robèd then in blood-washed linen,
    Now I'll sing thy sovereign grace.
Come, dear Lord, no longer tarry,
    Take my raptured soul away;
Send thine angels down to carry
    Me to realms of endless day.

If thou ever didst discover
    Unto me the Promised Land,
Bid me now the streams pass over,
    On the heavenly border stand.
Help surmount whate'er opposes,
    Unto thy embraces fly;
Speak the word thou didst to Moses,
    Bid me get me up and die.

                —*Robert Robinson.*

    The author of this hymn was won to a Christian
life under the preaching of George Whitefield. Out

"Prone to wander, Lord, I feel it;
Prone to leave the God I love"

of mere curiosity he went to hear the great evangelist, and afterwards wrote to him, " I confess it was
to spy the nakedness of the land I came — to pity
the folly of the preacher, the infatuation of the
hearers, and to abhor the doctrine.   I went pitying
the poor deluded Methodists, but came away envy-
ing their happiness."

This hymn, which with one exception is the only
one of his authorship that has lived to our time, has,
no doubt, had its great power in the personal element which pervades it.   His personal experience
he portrays in the second verse, —

" Jesus sought me when a stranger,
    Wandering from the fold of God;
He, to save my soul from danger,
    Interposed his precious blood."

There is a very touching story connected with
this hymn and its author, showing that a hymn,
which has burst forth from a loving Christian heart
as naturally as a fountain gurgles from the moun-
tain side, may afterwards come back as a thorn of
remorse to remind the author of the spiritual exile
into which he has wandered.

Long before the railroads, when public travel in
England was largely by stagecoach, a lady and gentleman who were strangers to each other were the
only travelers on the inside of one of these coaches.
The lady had been for some time poring over a single

page of a little book to which she referred frequently. Turning, at length, to her companion, who did not seem to be engaged in his attention other than to note the changing scenery through which they were passing, she held the open page toward him, and said: " May I ask your attention to this hymn, and ask you to favor me with your opinion of it? Do you know it?"

The hymn to which she had called his attention was,—

" Come, thou fount of every blessing."

The gentleman addressed glanced down the page, and his face flushed with confusion as he attempted to excuse himself from conversation on the merits of the hymn; but the lady ventured on another appeal.

" That hymn has given me so much pleasure," she said. " Its sentiments so touch me; indeed, I cannot tell you how much good it has done me. Don't you think it very good?"

" Madam!" said the stranger, bursting into tears, " I am the poor unhappy man who wrote that hymn many years ago, and I would give a thousand worlds, if I had them, to enjoy the feelings I then had."

Robert Hall said of Robinson: " He had a musical voice, and was master of all its intonations; he had wonderful self-passion, and could say *what* he

pleased, *when* he pleased, and *how* he pleased."
Like many another brilliant and versatile man, he
ran a wandering course and was "unstable as
water."

It was doubtless a meditation on this sad frailty
of his own nature that led him to write with pray-
erful tenderness, the verse,—

> " Oh! to grace how great a debtor
>   Daily I'm constrained to be;
> Let that grace, Lord, like a fetter,
>   Bind my wandering soul to thee.
> Prone to wander, Lord, I feel it;
>   Prone to leave the God I love;
> Here's my heart, Lord, take and seal it,
>   Seal it from thy courts above."

THE FIELD OF THE WORLD.

In the morning sow thy seed, and in the evening withhold not thine hand: for thou knowest not whether shall prosper, either this or that, or whether they both shall be alike good. — Ecclesiastes xi., 6.

JAMES MONTGOMERY

BOYLSTON. S. M. LOWELL MASON.

Sow in the morn thy seed;
  At eve hold not thy hand;
To doubt and fear give thou no heed,
  Broadcast it o'er the land.

Beside all waters sow,
  The highway furrows stock,
Drop it where thorns and thistles grow,
  Scatter it on the rock.

The good, the fruitful ground,
  Expect not here nor there,
O'er hill and dale, by plots 'tis found;
  Go forth, then, everywhere.

Thou know'st not which shall thrive,
  The late or early sown;
Grace keeps the precious germ alive,
  When and wherever strown:

And duly shall appear,
   In verdure, beauty, strength,
The tender blade, the stalk, the ear,
   And the full corn at length.

Thou canst not toil in vain:
   Cold, heat, and moist, and dry,
Shall foster and mature the grain
   For garners in the sky.

Thence, when the glorious end,
   The day of God, shall come,
The angel reapers shall descend,
   And heaven cry, " Harvest Home! "

                —*James Montgomery.*

Montgomery has been called the Cowper of the nineteenth century. Like Cowper, he contributed many beautiful sacred songs so inspired with Christian love and so free from service to any special dogma that they have won universal popularity. As Frederick Saunders says: " Being inspired by the religion of love, they are eminently designed to diffuse the love of religion."

Montgomery declared that his love of poetry was kindled in his heart by hearing Blair's *Grave* read to him in his school days. He began writing poetry at a very early age, and continued it through his long and useful life. It has been said of him that " his history affords a fine example of virtuous and successful perseverance, and of genius devoted to pure and noble ends. — not a feverish, tumultuous, and splendid career, like that of some greater poetical heirs of immortality, but a course ever brightening as it proceeded,— calm, useful, and happy."

The hymn we are studying had its inspiration, as we would naturally imagine, in the fields. One day in the month of February, 1832, the poet was traveling with a friend between Gloucester and Tewkesbury, when he noticed some women and girls working in a field lately plowed. They were stooping down in rows, but they could not be weeding. What were they doing? Then he was told that their work was called " dibbling," and that instead of throwing in the grain broadcast over the field, holes were pricked in straight lines, and into each of these holes two or three grains of wheat were dropped.

" Dibbling is unpoetical, and unpicturesque," said Montgomery. " Give me broadcast sowing." And then he began to think about sowing the good seed — the dibbling of Sunday-school teaching and visiting, here a little, there a little, and of the broadcast sowing of the preacher. For James Montgomery to have a new idea was to have a new poem, and so gradually his thoughts shaped themselves into verses, and the hymn,—

" Sow in the morn thy seed,"

was born. It was first sung at the Sheffield Sunday School Union, at a Whitsuntide gathering, in 1832, but has found its way to the ends of the earth.

James Montgomery's earlier days were often troublous and disturbed by persecution, for, gentle and sweet as are many of his hymns, this contemplative hymn-writer had a conscience as unbending and a spirit as full of fire as our own James Russell Lowell. His opposition to slavery and other wrongs of his time brought upon him political antagonism which consigned him to a dungeon. A volume of his poems was published under the unique and significant title of *Prison Amusements*.

His personal religious experience is supposed to have been told in his " Stranger and His Friend," which is one of the most beautiful of his sacred poems: --

" A poor wayfaring man of grief
  Hath often crossed me on my way,
Who sued so humbly for relief,
  That I could never answer ' Nay.'
I had no power to ask his name,
Whither he went, or whence he came,
Yet there was something in his eye
That won my love, I know not why.

" Once when my scanty meal was spread,
  He entered, not a word he spake, --
Just perishing for want of bread.
  I gave him all; he blessed it, brake

"Sita in the moon-thicket"

And ate,—but gave me part again.
Mine was an angel's portion then;
For while I fed with eager haste,
That crust was manna to my taste.

" I spied him where a fountain burst
    Clear from the rock; his strength was gone;
The heedless water mocked his thirst.
    He heard it, saw it hurrying on;
I ran to raise the sufferer up;
Thrice from the stream he drained my cup;
Dipt, and returned it running o'er.
I drank, and never thirsted more.

" 'Twas night; the floods were out; it blew
    A winter hurricane aloof;
I heard his voice abroad, and flew
    To bid him welcome to my roof.
I warmed, I clothed, I cheered my guest,
Laid him on my own couch to rest,
Then made the hearth my bed, and seemed
In Eden's garden while I dreamed.

" Stript, wounded, beaten, nigh to death,
    I found him by the highway side;
I roused his pulse, brought back his breath,
    Revived his spirit and supplied
Care, oil, refreshment; he was healed.
I had myself a wound concealed,
But from that hour forgot the smart,
And Peace bound up my broken heart.

" In prison cell I saw him next, condemned
    To meet a traitor's death at morn;
The tide of lying tongues I stemmed,
    And honored him 'midst shame and scorn.
My friendship's utmost zeal to try
He asked if I for him would die?
The flesh was weak, my blood ran chill,
But the free spirit cried, ' I will.'

" Then in a moment to my view
    The stranger darted from disguise;
The tokens in his hands I knew,
    My Saviour stood before my eyes!
He spake and my poor name he named:
' Of me thou hast not been ashamed;
These deeds shall thy memorial be;
Fear not, thou did'st them unto me.' "

When Montgomery was drawing near the close of life, his friend, Dr. Holland, was reading to him from his own hymns. Noticing that the poet was visibly affected, he desisted. " Read on," said the dying poet, " I am glad to hear you: the words recall the feelings which first suggested them; and it is good for me to feel affected and humbled by the terms in which I have endeavored to provide for the expression of similar religious experience, in others. As all my hymns embody some portions of the history of the joys or sorrows, the hopes and the fears, of this poor heart, so I cannot doubt that they will be found an acceptable vehicle of expression of the experience of many of my fellow-creatures who may be similarly exercised during the pilgrimage of their Christian life."

OUR PASCHAL LAMB.

Worthy is the Lamb that was slain to receive power, and riches, and wisdom, and strength, and honour, and glory, and blessing. — Revelation v., 12.

OUR PASCHAL LAMB.

AUTUMN, 8, 7. D. SPANISH MELODY. FROM MARECHIO.

Hail! thou once despisèd Jesus!
Hail! thou Galilean King!
Thou didst suffer to release us;
Thou didst free salvation bring.
Hail! thou universal Saviour!
Bearer of our sin and shame;
By thy merits we find favour:
Life is given through thy name.

Paschal Lamb, by God appointed,
All our sins on thee were laid;
By Almighty love anointed,
Thou hast full atonement made.

275

Every sin may be forgiven,
    Through the virtue of thy blood;
Opened is the gate of heaven:
    Peace is made 'twixt man and God.

Jesus, hail! enthron'd in glory,
    There forever to abide;
All the heavenly hosts adore thee,
    Seated at thy Father's side.
There for sinners thou art pleading;
    There thou dost our place prepare;
Ever for us interceding,
    Till in glory we appear.

Worship, honour, power, and blessing,
    Thou art worthy to receive;
Loudest praises, without ceasing,
    Meet it is for us to give.
Help, ye bright angelic spirits,
    Bring your sweetest, noblest lays;
Help to sing our Saviour's merits,
    Help to chant Immanuel's praise.

Soon we shall with those in glory
    His transcendent grace relate;
Gladly sing th' amazing story
    Of his dying love so great.
In that blessed contemplation,
    We for evermore shall dwell,
Crown'd with bliss and consolation,
    Such as none below can tell.

                    —*John Bakewell.*

This is the only hymn of Bakewell's that has survived the century and come down to our day, but
this beautiful salutation to Christ is so full of solemn
pathos as well as poetic beauty that Christians everywhere have written it in their books and on their
hearts until its immortality is assured. The hymn
is so truly catholic that it has crossed all denomina-
tional lines, and voices the love and devotion of all
who honor Christ.

The story is told of an old lover of this hymn,
that he had been sitting listening to a devoted
Christian woman, who, amidst great infirmity, was
reclining on her couch, chanting in sweet undertones, —

> " Jesus, hail! enthron'd in glory,
>> There forever to abide;
> All the heavenly hosts adore thee,
>> Seated at thy Father's side.
> There for sinners thou art pleading;
>> There thou dost our place prepare;
> Ever for us interceding,
>> Till in glory we appear."

Breaking off her song for a moment, she turned and
said, " Whose hymn is that? It is a precious one to
me. It keeps me the whole day sometimes, and
through wakeful hours at night, too, in communion
with my glorified Savior. Who wrote it?"

"It was written," was the reply, "in 1760, by John Bakewell."

"Bakewell, — Bakewell! Surely it may be the same as wrote a letter which I have read in one of the old magazines. I think the letter is in the volume for 1816. Just take it down from the shelf yonder and read it. It is about Christian brotherly love."

The letter was read. The good woman fixed upon some paragraphs as the more impressive to her mind; this among the rest: "I took the liberty of giving you my thoughts on brotherly love, and the unity which ought to subsist between the children of God. I have been confirmed in my opinions on these subjects by reading the fourth chapter of the Epistle to the Ephesians. This one point, the unity of the spirit, Paul presses with seven arguments. It is as if the Apostle should reason thus: If the church, your mother, be but one; God, your Father, one; Christ, your Lord, one; the Holy Ghost, your Comforter, one; if there be but one hope, one faith, and one baptism, it is certainly your bounden duty to live together in love as one, endeavoring to keep the unity of the spirit in the bond of peace."

"Now, I like that," said the good woman; "I like the spirit of it as well as the argument. Is the writer the same as he who wrote the hymn?"

"Yes."

"I am glad to know that. It is so like the man who taught me to sing,—

> "Soon we shall with those in glory
>   His transcendent grace relate;
> Gladly sing th' amazing story
>   Of his dying love so great.
> In that blessed contemplation
>   We for evermore shall dwell,
> Crown'd with bliss and consolation,
>   Such as none below can tell."

Bakewell lived to be ninety-eight years old, having preached the Gospel, at the time of his death, for full seventy years. His sermons have long since passed from the memory of men, but his beautiful hymn will carry his name and the fragrance of his reverent, loving soul from age to age.

And Jacob . . . took of the stones of that place, and put them for his pillows, ... and he dreamed, and behold a ladder set up on the earth, and the top of it reached to heaven: and behold the angels of God ascending and descending on it. And, behold, the Lord stood above it.— Genesis xxviii., 10 – 13.

"There let the way appear
Steps unto heaven"

NEARER TO GOD.

BETHANY. 6, 4, 6.   LOWELL MASON.

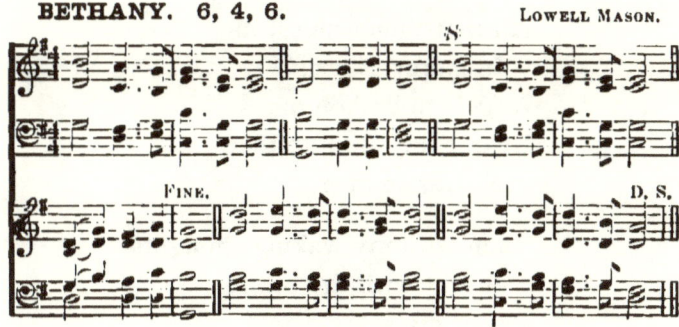

Nearer, my God, to thee,
  Nearer to thee!
E'en though it be a cross
  That raiseth me;
Still all my song shall be,
Nearer, my God, to thee,
  Nearer to thee!

Though like the wanderer,
  The sun gone down,
Darkness be over me,
  My rest a stone,—
Yet in my dreams I'd be
Nearer, my God, to thee,
  Nearer to thee!

There let the way appear
  Steps unto heaven;

All that thou sendest me,
   In mercy given;
Angels to beckon me
Nearer, my God, to thee,
   Nearer to thee!

Then with my waking thoughts
   Bright with thy praise,
Out of my stony griefs
   Bethel I'll raise;
So by my woes to be
Nearer, my God, to thee,
   Nearer to thee!

Or if, on joyful wing
   Cleaving the sky,
Sun, moon, and stars forgot,
   Upward I fly,—
Still all my song shall be,
Nearer, my God, to thee,
   Nearer to thee!

              —*Sarah Flower Adams.*

   This hymn, which has not only found its way into all hymn books of the English tongue, but has been translated into many foreign languages, was written as a record of personal religious experience and as a memorial of gratitude because the author's prayers had been answered. Like many another hymn that has become famous and universally helpful, it was the upspringing of gratitude in a reverent soul, and was written without any expectation that it would become a popular hymn.

It is a most beautiful study of Jacob's vision at Luz. In the second verse the young wandering Jacob, going out from home sad at heart, with a burden of sin upon him and all the future looking dark, and yet longing somehow to find his way back to God, is very strikingly portrayed,—

" Though like the wanderer,
    The sun gone down,
Darkness be over me,
    My rest a stone,—
Yet in my dreams I'd be
    Nearer, my God, to thee,
        Nearer to thee!"

And nothing could be finer than the spiritualizing of the old Scriptural record which tells the story of Jacob's waking in the morning, and realizing that even that lonely place was a Bethel to him because of the presence of God. Multitudes of burdened and sorrowing souls, lying down lonely in their desert, have been encouraged to mount up as with wings on her splendid song, —

" Then with my waking thoughts
    Bright with thy praise,
Out of my stony griefs
    Bethel I'll raise;

287

> So by my woes to be
> Nearer, my God, to thee,
> Nearer to thee! ''

This hymn is such a universal favorite that there
are many incidents telling of the good cheer and
comfort it has brought in times of trial. Bishop
Marvin relates that during the War of the Rebellion
he was once traveling in a wild region in Arkansas.
He had been driven from his home by the Union
troops, and was greatly depressed. But as he drew
near a dilapidated log cabin he heard some one
singing, '' Nearer, my God, to thee.'' He got down
from his horse and entered the house. There he
found an old widow woman singing in the midst of
such poverty as he had never before seen. His fears
and despondency vanished and he went on his way,
happy and trustful because of the faith which he
had beheld and the hymn which he had heard.

After the battle of Fort Donelson, as the hospital
corps went over the field searching for the wounded,
they discovered a little drummer-boy, one of the
many lads who ought to have been at home with
their mothers, but who in those awful days of car-
nage found their way in scores and hundreds to the
front. He had been fearfully wounded, one arm
having been entirely carried away by a cannon ball.
The brave boy died before they could carry him off
the field, but he kept up a cheerful heart and com-

forted himself by singing Mrs. Adams' precious
hymn. Up from the blood-stained battle-field, and
through the murky clouds of powder-smoke, rang
the half-childish voice, as he sang,—

> " There let the way appear
>   Steps unto heaven;
> All that thou sendest me
>   In mercy given;
> Angels to beckon me
> Nearer, my God, to thee,
>   Nearer to thee!"

This hymn is always sung by caravans of pilgrims
from Christian lands when, in making the tour of
Palestine, they camp at Bethel. It is surely a
sweet immortality for this Christian woman that
her song should thus linger about the Holy Land,
the stories of which were so dear to her, and continue to interpret the worshipful thoughts of Christian travelers long after she has gone to her reward.

The author died young, and the prayer of her
hymn was answered, in that she passed away from
earth with trustful song upon her lips, thus fulfilling
the glad expectation of the last verse of her noblest
poem,—

> " Or if, on joyful wing
>   Cleaving the sky,

Sun, moon, and stars forgot,
 Upward I fly,—
Still all my song shall be,
Nearer, my God, to thee,
 Nearer to thee!"

"STAND UP FOR JESUS."

Having done all, to stand. — Ephesians vi., 13.

GEORGE DUFFIELD

"STAND UP FOR JESUS."

WEBB. 7, 6.   GEORGE JAMES WEBB.

Stand up!—stand up for Jesus!
  Ye soldiers of the cross;
Lift high his royal banner,
  It must not suffer loss.
From victory unto victory
  His army shall he lead
Till every foe is vanquish'd,
  And Christ is Lord indeed.

Stand up!—stand up for Jesus!
  The solemn watchword hear;
If while ye sleep he suffers,
  Away with shame and fear;
Where'er ye meet with evil,
  Within you or without,
Charge for the God of Battles,
  And put the foe to rout!

Stand up! — stand up for Jesus!
  The trumpet call obey;
Forth to the mighty conflict,
  In this his glorious day.
" Ye that are men now serve him,"
  Against unnumbered foes;
Let courage rise with danger,
  And strength to strength oppose.

Stand up! — stand up for Jesus!
  Stand in his strength alone,
The arm of flesh will fail you,
  Ye dare not trust your own.
Put on the Gospel armor,
  Each piece put on with prayer;
Where duty calls, or danger,
  Be never wanting there!

Stand up! — stand up for Jesus!
  Each soldier to his post;
Close up the broken column,
  And shout through all the host!
Make good the loss so heavy,
  In those that still remain,
And prove to all around you
  That death itself is gain!

Stand up! — stand up for Jesus!
  The strife will not be long;
This day the noise of battle,
  The next the victor's song.

To him that overcometh,
A crown of life shall be;
He with the King of Glory
Shall reign eternally!

—George Duffield.

This is the most stirring and martial of all the hymns sung by the Christian Church in America. Its inspiration was a most tragic occurrence. The words chosen for the title, and repeated as the trumpet-call at the beginning of every verse, were the dying message of Rev. Dudley A. Tyng to the Young Men's Christian Association and the ministers associated with them in the Noon-day Prayer-meeting during the great revival of 1858, commonly known as the "Work of God in Philadelphia." Mr. Tyng had been the magnetic and consecrated leader of that historic revival campaign. On the Sabbath before his death, he preached, in the immense edifice known as Jaynes' Hall, a sermon which, judged by the greatest test of all — the number of souls won to Christ — was, perhaps, the most successful ever preached in America. His text was, "Go now, ye that are men, and serve the Lord." There were five thousand men listening to his fervent words, and it was believed that fully one thousand then and there yielded their wills to serve Christ and went away to lead Christian lives.

The following Wednesday the young minister left

his study for a moment, and went to the barn floor, where a mule was at work on a horsepower machine for shelling corn. Patting the animal on the neck, the sleeve of Mr. Tyng's silk study-gown caught in the cogs of the wheel, and he was so fearfully injured that he died within a few hours. It is doubtful if there was ever so great a lamentation over the death of a private citizen.

When told by his friends that he could not live, he turned to his physician and said: " Doctor, my friends have given me up; they say that I am dying; is that your opinion?" The doctor replied in the affirmative. " Then, doctor, I have something to say to you. I have loved you much as a friend; I long to love you as a brother in Jesus Christ. Let me entreat you now to come to Jesus."

His father, who was also a distinguished minister, asked if he had any message to his brethren in the ministry? He replied, " Father, stand up for Jesus. Tell them all to stand up for Jesus."

The Sunday following the death of Mr. Tyng, Dr. George Duffield preached from Ephesians, sixth chapter, and fourteenth verse, " Stand therefore, having your loins girt about with truth, and having on the breastplate of righteousness." For a concluding exhortation he had composed this hymn, which will be his greatest claim to immortality. The superintendent of the Sabbath-school had it printed on a little slip for the children; a stray copy

"Stand up! stand up for Jesus!
The trumpet call obey"

found its way into a newspaper, and it went on, and on, until it has been printed in all the leading languages of the world.

The martial words and spirit of the hymn made it a great favorite among the Christian soldiers during the War of the Rebellion. The first time the author heard it sung outside of his own denomination was in 1864, on a visit to the Army of the James.

It is said that Dr. Roberts, of Princeton, on a visit to Saratoga, took his little four-year-old child to church with him one Sunday morning. The hymn given out was,—

" Stand up!—stand up for Jesus!"

The baby happened to be very familiar with that hymn and began at once, in all simplicity and innocence, to sing it in a loud and joyful voice, at first to the astonishment, but finally to the admiration, of the congregation.

The author once wrote to a friend: "There is one pleasure I have enjoyed in hymns which is somewhat personal and of its own kind. On three different occasions—once in the General Assembly at Brooklyn, and once at a meeting of the A. B. F. M., and once at a mass-meeting of Sabbath-schools in Illinois, when outward and inward troubles met and I was in great and sore affliction—I have en-

tered the church and found that the great congregation was singing,—

'Stand up!—stand up for Jesus!'

The feeling of comfort was inexpressible, to have
my own hymn thus sung *to* me by those unaware
of my presence. It was as though an angel
strengthened me."

ON THE RESURRECTION.

On his head were many crowns.— Revelation
xix., 12.

CORONATION. C. M.   OLIVER HOLDEN.

All hail the power of Jesus' name!
  Let angels prostrate fall;
Bring forth the royal diadem,
  To crown him Lord of all!

Let high-born seraphs tune the lyre,
  And, as they tune it, fall
Before his face who tunes their choir,
  And crown him Lord of all!

Crown him, ye morning stars of light,
  Who fixed this floating ball;
Now hail the Strength of Israel's might,
  And crown him Lord of all!

307

Crown him, ye martyrs of your God,
    Who from his altar call;
Extol the stem of Jesse's rod,
    And crown him Lord of all!

Ye seed of Israel's chosen race,
    Ye ransomed of the fall,
Hail him who saves you by his grace,
    And crown him Lord of all!

Hail him, ye heirs of David's line,
    Whom David Lord did call,
The God incarnate, Man divine,
    And crown him Lord of all!

Sinners, whose love can ne'er forget
    The wormwood and the gall,
Go spread your trophies at his feet,
    And crown him Lord of all!

Let every tribe and every tongue
    That bound creation's call
Now shout in universal song,
    The crownèd Lord of all!

              —*Edward Perronet.*

Edward Perronet, the author of this, the most in-
spiring hymn in the English language, was a close
friend of the Wesleys, and shared with them their
hardships and their triumphs. "Mr. Perronet,"
says Charles Wesley, in a letter to a friend, "joins

in hearty love and thanks for your kind concern for him. He grows apace, is bold as a lion, and begins to speak in this Name to the hearts of sinners." A proof of his boldness and meekness in the service of his Divine Master is recorded by Mr. Wesley. " It was past eight," writes that singing evangelist, " when we came to Penkridge. We were hardly set down when the sons of Belial beset the house, and beat at the door. I ordered it to be set open, and immediately they filled the house. I sat still in the midst of them for half an hour. Edward Perronet I was a little concerned for, lest such rough treatment at his first setting out should daunt him; but he abounded in valor, and was for reasoning with the wild beasts before they had spent any of their violence. He got a deal of abuse thereby, and not a little dirt, both of which he took very patiently."

The young poet kept up this cheerful spirit despite all hardships; for, three years later, Charles Wesley put another jotting in his note-book concerning the now world-renowned author of " Coronation." He says: " I set out for London with my brother and Ned Perronet. We were in perils of robbers, who were abroad, and had robbed many the night before. We commended ourselves to God, and rode over the heath singing." What a trio that was on horseback that morning! John Wesley, Charles Wesley, and Edward Perronet!

How they have dispersed robber doubts, and fears,
and sorrows, by their glad songs, in every land!

Dr. Belcher relates that John Wesley had long
been desirous of hearing Edward Perronet preach;
and the latter, aware of it, was as resolutely determined that he should not, and therefore studied
to avoid every occasion that would lead to it. Mr.
Wesley was preaching in London one evening, and,
seeing Mr. Perronet in the chapel, announced, without asking his consent, that he would preach there
the next morning at five o'clock. Mr. Perronet
had too much respect for the congregation to dis-
turb their peace by a public remonstrance, and too
much regard for Mr. Wesley entirely to resist his
bidding. The night passed over. Mr. Perronet
ascended the pulpit under the impression that Mr.
Wesley would be secreted in some corner of the
chapel, if he did not show himself publicly, and,
after singing and prayer, informed the congregation
that he appeared before them contrary to his own
wish; that he had never been once asked, much less
his consent gained, to preach; that he had done violence to his feelings to show his respect for Mr.
Wesley; and, now that he had been compelled to
occupy the place in which he stood, weak and inade-
quate as he was for the work assigned him, he
would pledge himself to furnish them with the best
sermon that ever had been delivered. Opening the
Bible, he proceeded to read our Lord's Sermon on

the Mount, which he concluded without a single word of his own by way of note or comment. He closed the service with singing and prayer. Dr. Belcher declares that no imitator has been able to produce equal effect.

Mr. Perronet wrote the hymn which earned him immortality in 1779, and it was first published in the *Gospel Magazine*. Probably no hymn ever written is so universally sung to-day.

Many years ago a Methodist local preacher named William Dawson, a farmer, who was an original genius and a very striking and popular speaker, was preaching in London on the divine offices of Christ. After setting him forth as the great Teacher and Priest, he showed him in his glory as the King of saints. He proclaimed him as King in his own right, and then proceeded to the coronation. His ideas were borrowed from scenes familiar to his hearers. He graphically portrayed the marshalling of the immense procession. Then it moved towards the grand Temple to place the insignia of royalty upon the King of the universe. So vividly was all this depicted, that those who listened thought they were gazing upon a long line of patriarchs, kings, prophets, apostles, martyrs, and confessors of every age and clime. They saw the great Temple filled; and the grand and solemn act of coronation was about to be performed. By this time the congregation was wrought up to the highest pitch of excitement, and while expecting to hear the pealing anthem rise from the vast assembly upon which they seemed to gaze, the preacher lifted up his voice and sang,—

> " All hail the power of Jesus' name!
>   Let angels prostrate fall;
>   Bring forth the royal diadem,
>   To crown him Lord of all!"

The effect was overwhelming. The crowd sprang to their feet, and sang the hymn with a feeling and a power which seemed to swell higher and higher at every verse. " It was," says Rev. S. W. Christophers, who relates the incident, " a jubilant multitude paying harmonious homage to their Sovereign Lord and Saviour."

Rev. E. P. Scott, while a missionary in India, one day on the street of a village met a very strange-looking native who proved to be from an interior tribe of warlike mountaineers that had never heard the Gospel. The missionary at once prepared to visit this wild tribe, taking with him, among other things, his violin. His friends urged that he was exposing himself to needless peril, but his reply was, " I must carry Jesus to them." After two days of travel, he was suddenly confronted by a war party of the tribe which he sought. They had been lying in ambush and sprang out menacingly in his path, pointing their spears at his heart. Expecting nothing but instant death, he drew out his violin, shut his eyes, and commenced to play and sing,—

" All hail the power of Jesus' name!"

When he reached the verse, beginning,—

" Let every tribe and every tongue,"

he opened his eyes and found the wild children of the forest on their knees at his feet. It was the beginning of a residence of over two years, and the entire tribe were won to Christ.

We can scarcely conceive a better hymn than this to sing in heaven, when all the ransomed throng are gathered to do honor to our Divine Lord.